HISTORY
of the
BARCLAY/BARKLEY CLAN

ROGER DE BERCHELAI
SCOTLAND

Barber/Barbour Genealogy: Book 1

Compiled by

Betty Jewell Durbin Carson

DAR Member #832584

HERITAGE BOOKS
2016

HERITAGE BOOKS

AN IMPRINT OF HERITAGE BOOKS, INC.

Books, CDs, and more—Worldwide

For our listing of thousands of titles see our website
at
www.HeritageBooks.com

Published 2016 by
HERITAGE BOOKS, INC.
Publishing Division
5810 Ruatan Street
Berwyn Heights, Md. 20740

International Standard Book Numbers
Paperbound: 978-0-7884-5718-0
Clothbound: 978-0-7884-6451-5

Acknowledgement

I would like to give acknowledgement to my sister, Doris May Durbin Wooley, who worked with me on this research of the Barber/Barbour and Barclay/Barkley families for over 15 years. We visited many state archives, courthouses, bought and Xeroxed many documents, searched census records, and loved doing it as a team.

Doris died February 4, 2014, but left me all of her notes and files which I combined with mine. The Barber line is closely intermarried with the Barclay/Barkley family for many years. This book is dedicated to our deceased mother, Nellie Barkley Durbin, as it is part of her ancestry.

While there has not been any definite proof that Thomas and Samuel were related, available records would indicate a close connection. Thomas had a younger brother named Samuel and this Samuel may be a grandson or nephew. Many of the names in Thomas' manuscript as well as Samuel's have names that are connected through DNA lines.

That is why there are two Barber books. Records indicate that the American progenitor was Francis Barber, 1616/17, b. England, perhaps the one who came to VA in 1635; children: Francis 165?; Samuel 1955 m. Elizabeth Heathcoate; John; Sarah; Elizabeth; Joseph; and William 166?

Nellie Barkley Durbin - 1948

Nellie Barkley as a young woman

Towie-Barclay Castle

- **Arms** – Azure, a chevron Or between three crosses pattee Argent
- **Badge** - Within a strap, a chapeau Azure doubled Ermine, a hand holding a dagger Proper.
- **Motto** – Aut agere aut mori – "Either action or death."
- **Dress Tartan**- Yellow and black with white overcheck.
- **Hunting Tartan** – Blue and green with red overcheck.
- **Standard** – Measuring 12 feet long, this standard was approved by the Lord Lyon's Office and is for the Chief's personal use. Azure, a St. Andrew's Cross Argent in the hoist and of two tracts Azure and or, upon which is depicted the Crest three times along with the Motto 'Aut agere aut mori' in letters Gules upon two transverse bands Argent.
- **Pinsel** - Authorized by our Chief to be flown by his Commissioner for North America at activities in the United States and Canada when the Chief is unable to be in attendance. Or, displaying the Crest within a strap Azure, inscribed in letters Or with the Motto 'Aut agere aut mori' all within a circlet Or, fimbriated Azure, ensigned of a chapeau Azure furred Ermine, inscribed with the title 'Barclay of that Ilk' in letters Azure, and in the fly an Escrol Azure bearing in the letters Or this slogan 'Towie Barclay' surmounting a stem of mayflower Proper.
- **Plant Badge** – a stem of mayflower Proper.
- **Lands** – Kincardinshire, Aberdeenshire, Banffshire, and Ayrshire
- **Origin of name** – Place-name from Berkeley, Gloucestershire, England

This brief historical overview of the surname is the official history of the surname and is made available by Clan Barclay International. More information and details of family history can be obtained from: Barclay, Leslie. *The History of the Scottish Barclays*, reprinted with an index and glossary by Carolyn L. Barkley, FSA Scot (Willow Bend Books, 1995) and Barclay, Hubert F., Charles W. Barclay and Alice Wilson-Fox. *A History of the Barclay Family,* 2 vol. (reprint, 1924-1933, Willow Bend Books, 2003).

Roger de Berchelai came to England with William the Conqueror and was granted Berkeley Castle in Gloucestershire. This early form of the name was believed to be the Anglo-Saxon version of 'beau' meaning beautiful, and 'lee', a meadow or field. Roger was mentioned in the Domesday Book as well as his son, John. In 1069 John de Berchelai accompanied Margaret (later St. Margaret) to Scotland. In gratitude for his service, King Malcolm (Canmore) granted him the lands of Towie, near Turriff, in Aberdeenshire, as well as the title, Barclay of that Ilk. 900 years of Barclay history in Scotland descend from John's three sons, Walter, Alexander, and Richard.

In the early days of violence, there was a black day when a nunnery was plundered by the Towie Barclays. Following this event, Thomas the Rhymer wrote the following lines:

"Towie Barclay of the Glen, Happy to the maids, But never to the men."

This curse was said to haunt the male-heir. It was a belief held so strongly that in 1755, it was given as a reason for the heir's sale of Towie Barclay Castle, which then passed into the keeping of the Governors of Robert Gordon's Hospital in Aberdeen. No Barclays have lived in the Castle since.

The Barclays formed important alliances and held land throughout the northeast of Scotland, principally Towie, Mathers, Gartley and Pierston in Aberdeenshire. They also settled in Banff, Collairnie in Fife, Brechin in Forfarshire and Stonehaven in Kincardineshire. One family line settled on the west coast in the Ardrossan and Kilbirnie areas in Ayrshire. Throughout Scotland, they played important roles in national affairs. Sir David Barclay was one of Robert the Bruce's chief associates and was present at many of his battles. Sir Walter de Berkeley, Gartley III, Lord Redcastle and Inverkeillor, was Great Chamberlain of Scotland, 1165-1189. Alexander de Berkeley, Gartley IX, became Mathers I in 1351 when he married Katherine Keith, sister of the Earl Marischal. Their son Alexander was the first to adopt the Barclay form of the surname. Sir George Barclay, Gartley XIX, was Steward of the household of Mary, Queen of Scots, and a later Sir George was second in command of James IV forces in the Highlands in the 1689.

One of the major Barclay families was established at Urie near Stonehaven in Kincardineshire. The first Laird, Colonel David Barclay, was a professional soldier serving with such armies as that of Gustavus Adolphus. He returned home when civil war broke out and serviced as a colonel of a regiment of horse fighting for the king. Following his retirement and the conclusion of the war, he was confined in Edinburgh Castle where he was converted to the Society of Friends (Quakers). His son Robert, Urie II, was widely known for his *Apologia*, described on the title page as being an *Explanation and Vindication of the Principles and Doctrines of the People called Quakers*. It was published in 1659 when Robert was twenty-seven, becoming widely influential, was then translated into all the European languages. He was friends with the leading Quakers of his day, George Fox and William Penn. Together, they were responsible for the idea of a city of brotherly love to be built in America. Instrumental in settling the east coast of the American colonies, Robert was appointed life governor by the proprietors of East New Jersey who granted him 5,000 acres of land. Robert's second son, David, left Urie and went to London and was apprenticed to a city company where he became a merchant and a rich man. His second wife was the daughter of John Fream, goldsmith, whose premises in Lombard Street became a banking center as the site of the Barclay's Bank. Wealth, however, did not corrupt the family's strict Quaker principles. David acquired an estate in Jamaica, freeing the slaves there and teaching them trades many years before the passing of laws against the institution of slavery. He entertained George III at his house in London for one of the Lord Mayor's processions, and he and his family were excused from kneeling to the King due to their Quaker beliefs. He refused a knighthood and preferment for his son at Court saying that 'He preferred to bring up his sons in honest trades'.

The last Laird of Urie, Captain Robert Barclay-Allardyce (Allardyce added when he married an heiress of that name whose lands were added to those of Urie), was known as the Great Pedestrian. Many tales exists of his walks over the Scottish hills, such as his walk from Urie to Crathynaird (28 miles), staying less than an hour and then walking home again the same day. His most famous record, however, was that of walking 1,000 miles in 1,000 hours. This he accomplished over a measured mile on Newmarket Heath, subject of about 100,000 wagers and before large crowds. This feat was accomplished in 1809 and five days later, he embarked with his regiment for the Walcheren Expedition in the Napoleonic Wars.

In 1621, Sir Patrick Barclay (Towie XVII) issued a letter of safe conduct for John and Peter Barclay, merchants in the town of Banff to settle in Riga on the shores of the Baltic where they became silk merchants and burghers. He was created a Prince by the Czar and his portrait hangs in the Hermitage in St. Petersburg. From them was founded the Russian line. Michael Andreas Barclay, born 1761, and descended from Peter, the original immigrant, entered the Russian Army with his two brothers. By 1806, Michael was in command of one of the Russian divisions sent to support Prussia against the French. He gained distinction at the battles of Wagram and Eylau. At the later, he had his horse shot out from under him and was severely wounded. He was made Minister of War in 1810 and two years later was given command of the Russian Armies against Napoleon. He invented the policy of 'scorched earth', retreating and hiburning until starvation and cold forced Napoleon into the terrible retreat from Moscow. In 1815, Michael was elevated by the Czar to Field Marshal Prince Michael Barclay de Tolly and was made a Count of the Holy Roman Empire. From England, George III bestowed upon him a G.C.B. The Prince came to London to receive this honor and met Colonel Sir Robert Barclay (Towie XXV) to whom he declared himself to be 'perfectly acquainted with his descent from the Barclays of Towie in Scotland'.

Portrait of Barclay de Tolly:

Map of East & West Jersey, titled:

EAST AND WEST JERSEY 1664-1702

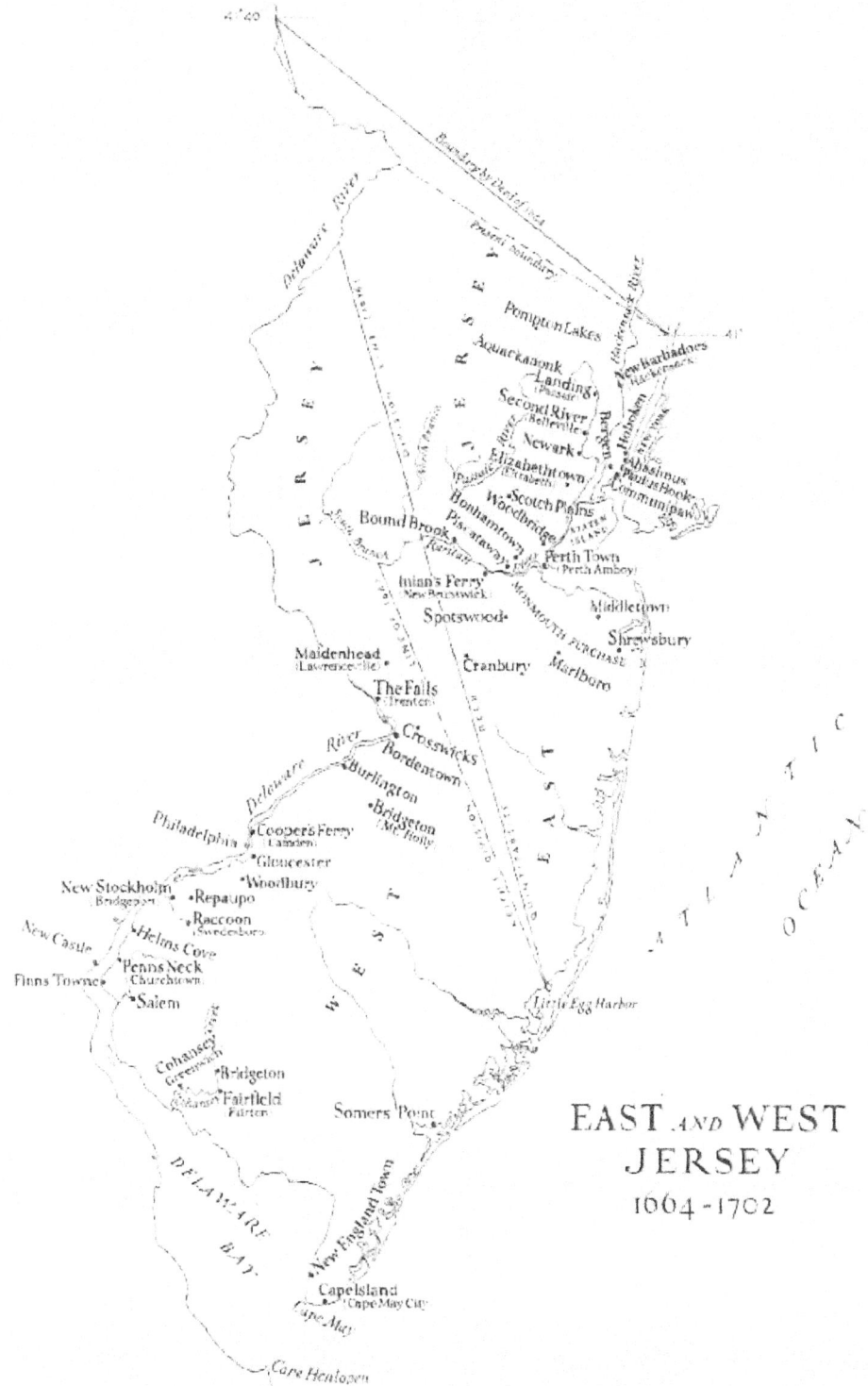

Places shown on map:

- Pompton Lakes
- Aquackanonk
- Landing (Passaic)
- New Barbadoes (Hackensack)
- Second River (Belleville)
- Hoboken
- Newark
- Bergen
- Weehawken
- Paulus Hook
- New York
- Elizabethtown (Elizabeth)
- Communipaw
- Scotch Plains
- Bonhamtown
- Woodbridge
- Piscataway
- Staten Island
- Bound Brook
- Raritan
- Perth Town (Perth Amboy)
- Inian's Ferry (New Brunswick)
- Middletown
- Spotswood
- Shrewsbury
- Maidenhead (Lawrenceville)
- Cranbury
- Marlboro
- The Falls (Trenton)
- Crosswicks
- Bordentown
- Burlington
- Bridgeton (Mt. Holly)
- Philadelphia
- Cooper's Ferry (Camden)
- Gloucester
- Woodbury
- New Stockholm (Bridgeport)
- Repaupo
- Raccoon (Swedesboro)
- New Castle
- Helms Cove
- Penns Neck (Churchtown)
- Finns Towne
- Salem
- Little Egg Harbor
- Cohansey (Greenwich)
- Bridgeton
- Fairfield (Fairton)
- Somers Point
- New England Town
- Capeisland (Cape May City)
- Cape May
- Cape Henlopen

Rivers and bodies of water: Delaware River, Hackensack River, Passaic River, Raritan River, Delaware Bay, Atlantic Ocean

Boundaries noted: Boundary by Deed of 1664, Present Boundary, Monmouth Purchase

Table of Contents

David Barclay of Urie, Scotland

Descendants of David Barclay of Urie

Generation No. 1

1. DAVID BARCLAY OF[1] URIE was born 1610, and died October 12, 1686 in Ury, Scotland. He married KATHERINE GORDON December 24, 1647 in Ury, Scotland.

Notes for DAVID BARCLAY OF URIE:
He served with distinction in the "Thirty Years War" as a follower of Gustavus Adolphus. He purchased in 1648, the estate of Ury in county of Kincardine, Scotland. In 1679, under charter from the Crown, this estate and some neighboring estates were united into the barony of Ury. Until some time preceding the purchase of Ury, and for a period of more than five hundred years, the family had owned and been identified with the estate of Mathers. In 1666, Colonel David Barclay joined the Society of Friends, and, as a consequence, was subjected to persecution, imprisonment, and frequent indignities. He married, December 24, 1647, Lady Katherine Gordon, known as the "White Rose of Scotland."

More About DAVID BARCLAY OF URIE:
Burial: October 12, 1686

Children of DAVID URIE and KATHERINE GORDON are:
      i.   DAVID[2] BARCLAY.

         Notes for DAVID BARCLAY:
         Barclay, David (Grantee) to David Barclay; East Jersey Proprietors. Warrant: 4,000 acres. Upon of Cheesequake Creek. To D. Barclay. Part of promised "2,000 acres for each of the said Proprietors at Present." Also, Barclay, David (Grantee) to David Barclay; Scots Proprietors. Warrant: 1,000 acres. East Side of Cheesequake Creek, "In behalf of himself (David Barclay) and the Proprietors belonging to Scotland"; part of promised 2,000 acres for eah of the said Proprietors at Present." 3 July 1684.

         Barclay, David, Jr. (deceased, brother of John, Late of Way, Scotland). To Andrew Hamilton (Merchant of Edinburgh, Scotland). From John Barclay of Perth Amboy, brother and administrator of David. Conveyance: 10 acres. Perth Amboy, Middlesex County. 12 August 1686.

         Barclay, David (Grantor) to John Barclay; from David Barclay; Robert Barclay. Conveyance: Unrecorded, East Jersey. 8 March 1686.

         Barclay, John (Grantee) to John Barclay. Survey: 250 acres. Crosswicks Creek (where the Partition line crosses the Creek). For J. Barclay "in Right of a [20th] part of a Propriety" Bordering lands "Late of Anthony Woodward"; and lands of P. Sonmans. Survey undated. Also, 500 acres. Monmouth (along the Birlington path in the way to Middleton). For J. Barclay. The property was waived. David Barclay, Jr. died in 1685 on his voyage from Scotland to Perth Amboy. Others named: David Barclay, Jr. (deceased, brother of John, Late of Way, Scotland); John Campbell (Land Agent of Andrew Hamilton in Perth Amboy); Lawrie (Governor, owner of adjacent land); Scots Proprietors; East Jersey.
         See also: Book B; folio 42. L(EJ): Folio 119 (PEASJ003). 16 July 1686.

      ii.   JEAN BARCLAY, m. SIR EWEN CAMERON.
2.   iii.   JOHN BARCLAY, b. Kincardineshire, Scotland.
      iv.   LUCY BARCLAY.
      v.   ROBERT BARCLAY, b. 1648; d. 1690.

         Notes for ROBERT BARCLAY:
         The celebrated apologist of the Quakers.

Generation No. 2

2. JOHN[2] BARCLAY *(DAVID BARCLAY OF[1] URIE)* was born in Kincardineshire, Scotland. He married CATHERINE.

Child of JOHN BARCLAY and CATHERINE is:

3.   i.   GEORGE[3] BARKLEY, b. 1730, Monmouth County, New Jersey; d. February 1781, Washington County, Pennsylvania.

Generation No. 3

3. GEORGE[3] BARKLEY *(JOHN[2] BARCLAY, DAVID BARCLAY OF[1] URIE)* was born 1730 in Monmouth County, New Jersey, and died February 1781 in Washington County, Pennsylvania. He married AGNES GRANT 1749 in Pennsylvania. She was born 1732.

Notes for GEORGE BARKLEY:
Barclay of Barkley, George, Bk 1, pg. 20, Monongahela Co., PA: WIFE Agnes & children; Sarah, Thomas, Joseph, John, Hugh, James, George and William. Executors: sons John and Hugh. Witnesses: John Barkley, Hugh Barkley and Margaret Mafeet. Dated: June 18, 1781; Proven: November 28, 1781. (Will Book 1 - 1773-1811 [Extracts] Westmoreland County, PA; #15 (#36).

Notes for AGNES GRANT:
Grant, Andrew, Imported toNeill Campbell (Lord), December 1685, East Jersey. [A: Folio 225 (SSTSE023), New Jersey State Archives].

Grant, David, grantor, to Thomas Burgie, Bernardstown, Somerset County, New Jersey. May 20, 1767 [E-3: Folio 304 (SSTSE023)]

Grant, John, Grantee, to John Grant, from John Penn (by attorneys), Richard Penn; Thomas Penn. Basking Ridge, Somerset County, New Jersey. [K-2: Folio 248 (SSTSE023).

Grant, Ralph, (blacksmith) imported May 15, 1685; East New Jersey, servant imported by William Dockwra in February 1684/85 and registered August 13, 1685.

Children of GEORGE BARKLEY and AGNES GRANT are:

        i.   JOHN G.[4] BARKLEY, b. 1750, Bedford, Bedford County, Virginia; d. July 31, 1814, Washington County, Pennsylvania.
       ii.   JOHN TALBOTT BARKLEY, b. 1752, Bedford, Bedford County, Virginia; d. July 31, 1814, Washington County, Pennsylvania.
4.   iii.   HUGH BARKLEY, b. April 25, 1760, Somerset, New Jersey; d. May 22, 1830, Finleyville, Washington County, Pennsylvania.
5.   iv.   JOSEPH BARKLEY, b. April 25, 1760, Somerset, Somerset, Pennsylvania; d. 1845, Paris, Edgar, Illinois.
6.   v.   SARAH BARKLEY, b. 1769.
      vi.   JAMES BARKLEY, b. 1770.
     vii.   WILLIAM BARKLEY, b. February 21, 1770, Pigeon Creek, Washington County, Pennsylvania; d. September 27, 1833, Clermont County, OH.
    viii.   THOMAS BARKLEY, b. 1777.
7.   ix.   WILLIAM BARKLEY, b. 1774, Pigeon Creek, Washington County, Pennsylvania; d. September 27, 1833, Clermont County, OH.
      x.   HENRY BARKLEY, b. 1779.
     xi.   KATHERINE BARKLEY.
     xii.   MARY B. BARKLEY.

Generation No. 4

4. HUGH[4] BARKLEY (GEORGE[3], JOHN[2] BARCLAY, DAVID BARCLAY OF[1] URIE) was born April 25, 1760 in Somerset, New Jersey, and died May 22, 1830 in Finleyville, Washington County, Pennsylvania. He married ELIZABETH KIRKPATRICK, daughter of ANDREW KIRKPATRICK and MARGARET GASTON. She was born February 23, 1769 in Haskinagridge, Somerset, New Jersey, and died September 29, 1849 in Finleyville, Washington County, Pennsylvania.

Notes for HUGH BARKLEY:
Pvt. Hugh Barckley: Sons of the American Revolution, Pennsylvania Society George Washington Chapter, Revolutionary War Soldiers, 2014. Hugh and Elizabeth are buried in Mingo cemetery, where white marble tombstones stand in their memory.
Pictures of graves on "Find A Grave."

Will Book 4, page 514-515: "In the name of God amin I Hugh Barkley of Nottingham Township and Washington County and state of Pennsylvania being fare advanced in life and noting that all of men must die do think it proper to make this my last Will and Testament in maner and form folering in the first place doe recomend my soul to God who gave it me through the ritiousness of Jesus Christ our Lord and Savor and my body to the cinderid earth to be buried in a cristian like maner at the descretion of my excutors hearin after mentioned and as soon as convenient after my death . . . in the first place I Will and bequeath unto my beloved wife Elizabeth Barkley the third part of the remainder of my movabel property and one third of the rest of my estate together with her bed and beding as longe as she remain my widow and if she maries again not to have any of the profits of my reil estate and secondly my daughter Marget not fit to take care of herself she is to be maintained of my real estate to live with hir mother and if she should out live the mother than to have hir choice which of the brothers or sisters she will live with and that one is to have of my real estate what will ceape hir dessent and if their should be any want all my children except Jane McClain to pay eqaly for that purpose and as some of my children have received one hundred dolars each my daughter Mary Cheeseman and my daughter Martheo McMulen and my daughter Elizabeth Alison and daughter Isley Clarke have received to the amount of one hundred dolars and my son William has received his in part the rest of the hundred dolars is to be paid up to him and then my daughter Hanner is to have one hundred dolars paid up to ir and then my daughter Nancey is to have one hundred dolars paid up to hir and my son Hugh Barkley is to have out of the estate one hundred dolars if he stase at home till he is of age and if not onley to have a horse beast worth fifty dolars and my daughter Jane McClain to have not any thing more than she has got unless she should out live my daughter Marget and their should be any thing left after the legasys above specifid is paid and any thing left after Marget maintainnene then Jane to have an equal share of what may be left and farther my grand daughter Mariah Colwell if she stase with us til of age is have of my estate a bed and beding and one sow and hir cloaths that is then on hand and farther it is my will at the death of my wife that my land be soald or if she should marrey it be soald and all them after the above legacys are paid all to share equal of the balance if any left after Marget mantainnence and farther I wish no inventory to be taken of my cloathe but that they be equally divid between my two sons William and Hugh Barkleys and lastly doe I anominat and appoint my beloved wife Elizabeth Barkley to execute this my last will in full as if I were hear to do it myself in testimony as this being my last will I have hereunto set my hand and seal this twenty ninth day of January one thousand eight hundred and thirty. Hugh Barkley {seal}. Test: Samuel Morgan, Samuel Gaston. Probated January 29, 1830.
Washington County, Pennsylvania. [Pennsylvania, Wills and Probates, 1683-1993]

More About ELIZABETH KIRKPATRICK:
Burial: Mingo Cemetery

Children of HUGH BARKLEY and ELIZABETH KIRKPATRICK are:
    i.   MARGARET[5] BARCKLEY, b. January 07, 1788.

          Notes for MARGARET BARCKLEY:
          Invalid, died unmarried.

    ii. MARY BARCKLEY, b. March 13, 1789; m. JOHN CHEESEMAN.
    iii. JANE BARCKLEY, b. March 15, 1791; m. (1) MR. CALDWELL; m. (2) ANDREW MCCLAIN.

          Notes for JANE BARCKLEY:
          Moved to Ohio

    iv.   SARA BARCKLEY, b. November 15, 1791; m. WILLIAM CLARK.
    v.   MARTHA BARCKLEY, b. February 19, 1793; m. JOHN MCMILLAN.
    vi.   ELIZABETH BARCKLEY, b. January 10, 1795; m. BEN ALLISON.

        Notes for ELIZABETH BARCKLEY:
        Lived in Ohio.

    vii.   WILLIAM BARCKLEY, b. March 13, 1799; m. POLLY ALLISON.
    viii.   ANN BARCKLEY, b. December 1800; d. Infant.
    ix.   ANDREW BARCKLEY, b. November 29, 1801; d. 1816.
    x.   HANNAH BARCKLEY, b. December 15, 1803; m. ALEXANDER CAMERON.
    xi.   NANCY KIRKPATRICK BARCKLEY, b. January 06, 1806; m. WILLIAM MURPHY.
    xii.   SUSANNAH BARCKLEY, b. November 18, 1808; d. 1822.
    xiii.   HUGH BARCKLEY, JR., b. January 13, 1811; d. July 28, 1878; m. MARY MURPHY.

5. JOSEPH[4] BARKLEY *(GEORGE[3], JOHN[2] BARCLAY, DAVID BARCLAY OF[1] URIE)* was born April 25, 1760 in Somerset, Somerset, Pennsylvania, and died 1845 in Paris, Edgar, Illinois. He married MARVILLA OR MARTHA 1790. She was born 1777, and died July 25, 1834 in Edgar, Illinois.

Children of JOSEPH BARKLEY and MARVILLA MARTHA are:

	i.	WILLIAM[5] BARKLEY, b. 1791.
8.	ii.	HUGH BARKLEY, b. 1794, Washington County, Pennsylvania; d. 1860, Effingham, Illinois.
	iii.	MARY BARKLEY, b. 1794; m. BENJAMIN DUGAN; b. November 30, 1810, Pleasant, Brown County, Ohio; d. December 05, 1870, Pleasant, Brown County, Ohio.
	iv.	SARAH BARKLEY, b. 1794; m. ELIAS THOMAS, July 08, 1831, Edgar County, Illinois.
9.	v.	GEORGE BARKLEY, b. April 12, 1795, Virginia; d. March 20, 1864, Effingham, Illinois.
	vi.	MARY BARKLEY, b. 1797.
10.	vii.	ANDREW BARKLEY, b. November 14, 1799, Pennsylvania; d. July 31, 1879, Symes, Edgar County, Illinois.
	viii.	JAMES S. BARKLEY, b. 1809, Pennsylvania; m. MARY HAWKINS, August 31, 1833, Edgar County, Illinois; b. 1819, Kentucky.
11.	ix.	JOHN B. BARKLEY, b. July 24, 1815, Clermont County, OH; d. October 31, 1931, Mayhill, Otero, New Mexico.

6. SARAH[4] BARKLEY *(GEORGE[3], JOHN[2] BARCLAY, DAVID BARCLAY OF[1] URIE)* was born 1769. She married JOHN FINLEY.

Children of SARAH BARKLEY and JOHN FINLEY are:
    i.   ROBERT[5] FINLEY.
    ii.   LEVI FINLEY.

7. WILLIAM[4] BARKLEY *(GEORGE[3], JOHN[2] BARCLAY, DAVID BARCLAY OF[1] URIE)* was born 1774 in Pigeon Creek, Washington County, Pennsylvania, and died September 27, 1833 in Clermont County, OH. He married REBECCA NEWKIRK 1819, daughter of HENRY NEWKIRK and CATHERINE. She was born 1774 in Pennsylvania, and died February 25, 1834 in Clermont County, OH.

Notes for WILLIAM BARKLEY:
Deed Book E4, page 222: March 28, 1806. John

WILLIAM BARKLEY
At a official meeting of the associate Judges of the Court of Common Pleas for the County of Clermont held at the Clerks office in the town of Balavia in said County on the 3rd day of December A. D. 1833 for the purpose of proving the will of William Barkley.

Present:

The honorable Robert Haines, Samuel Whitaker and John Emery associate Judges. This day the last Will and Testament of William Barkley, late of the County, deceased, was produced in Court. At the same time came Dawty Utter and James Bennett the subscribing witnesses, thereto who being duly sworn despose and say that they signed their names as witnesses as said will in the presence and at the request of the said Testator, the said William Barkley, that said Testator in their presence signed said Will and Published and pronounced the same as his last will and Testament, and that they believed the Testator was of full age, of sound and disposing mind, memory and Judgement and not under any restraint at the time of presenting said will whereupon the Court ordered said will be recorded.

Will to Wit

In the name of God Amen, I William Barkley, of the County of Clermont and State of Ohio, being of full age, and of sound mind and memory do make and dictate this to be my last Will and Testament as follows to Wit. Item 1st. It is my wish and desire that all my just debts which are but few, shall first be paid. Item 2nd: Whereas my sons, namely James, Henry, John and Joseph Barkley have each of them received in advance five hundred dollars and my daughters Katharine, wife of John F. McKiney has received the sum of three hundred dollars in advance, it is therefore my wish and desire that she shall receive the sum of two hundred dollars more, of the proceeds of my Estate. Item 3rd: And further it is my wish and desire that my daughter Polly Barkley, shall receive the sum of five hundred dollars from the proceeds of my Estate so as to make theim all equal. Item 4th: It is further my desire that the above money shall be raised by sale of my personal property and the residue to be disposed of as hereafter mentioned; and further there is a note at hand which I hold against Elizabeth Barkley wife of my son James Barkley, bearing date 21st day of September 1833, which it is my desire shall not be collected until a final settlement of all my personal property is made and then it is to be accounted for out of her part of the residue. Item 5th: It is further my wish and desire and I do hereby give and bequeth unto my grand daughter Rebecca Emeline Barkley, daughter of my son James Barkley, my dunn mare which is to be given in her Mother's possession immediately for safe keeping until she is of age, then to be given up to her and also I give and bequeath unto her one hundred dollars which is to be paid to her by my son Henry Barkley at the final settlement of my real estate, which hundred dollars is to come out of my son Henry Barkley"s Estate. Item 6th: And further it is my wish and desire that my wife Rebeccky shall have and hold all my real estate until her death likewise all the residue of my personal property after the above bequeaths are compiled with, and at her death it is my desire that all my Estate both real and personal shall be equally divided amongst all my children, namely the widdow of my son James and Henry, John and Joseph, Katareine and Polly Barkley. Item 7th: I wish it to be fully understood that I do wish and appoint my sons John and Joseph Barkley as my Executors to carry into effect this my Will and Testament given under my hand this 22nd day of September, 1833.

William Barkley
Attest:
Dawty Utter
James Bennett

On motion the Court order that letters Testamentary issue on said will to John Barkley and Joseph Barkley the Executors named therein on this entering into Bond in Fourteen hundred dollars with James Bennett and Dawty Utter their securities. Thereupon the said Executors with their securities entered into bond conditioned as the Law directs. The said Executors in open Court took the oath required by Law. The Court appoints Rudolph Cook, John Buckomon and Jacob Iher (?) appraiser of said Estate

Nathaniel Barber, Joseph Brown and William Eregon appraised the estate of William McKinney, late of Miami, township of Clermont County, Ohio. Amount of ---- page$ 21.09
First page 229.00
Second page 170.31 ½
Third page   45.75
Total $469.06 ½
Mentions Jacob McKinney a note not paid. Said to be in desperate circumstances. Note given to Henry Haskem by Jacob McKinney date 9th of November 1815 for $38.00. Due for John Ramsey to the estate $25.00.

A list of the goods belonging to the Estate of William McKinney, late of the County of Clermont. Deceased sold at Public sale by the undersigned administraors of the said Estate on the 20th day of September AD 1822.

To whom sold   Article   Price
Chaarley Loper + One lythe .56 1/4
William D trip + two singletrees .62 1/2
Isaac Riggs +paid to Est One iron wedge .62 1/2
Andrew Fryburger+ one lythe in ---- . 40
Haromon Eveland - lythe & cradle 1.75
Elsy Mc Kinney + one bull plow 2. 6 4/9
Samuel Wood + one frying pan . 43 3/4
elsy McKinney + one 10 gallon kittle 1. 75

Samuel Wood + one small d- .81
$9. 02 4/9
Abraham Miller + one big wheel   1.50
Widow   + one tool   .25
Widow   + one axe   1.50
Abraham Miller + one sled   .18 3/4
David Hammon   one pistol --pay   .75
William D. Trip + ---musket 2.80
Samuel Opdike + feed ----   .75
Samuel Opdike + one pair g---   .25
Samuel Wood + one spinning wheel + 2. 81 1/4
Widow   One loom 5.00
Lewis Fryburger to trip + one chain 1.41
Widow   + 2 chairs   .65
"   + 2 chairs   . 40
"   + 2 "   50
"   + 1 chair   .25
"   + 1 table   .50
"   + 1 bell   .35
Christopher Jorden +   seed hog   6.75
Jesse Smith + choice of 2 hogs   2. 12 1/2
Andrew Fryburger+   " "   2.00
John Ramsey +   " "   1.43 3/4
    " + " "   1. 37 1/2
Harmond Eveland +   " "   1.30
$35. 26
William D. Trip + 2 hogs 6th choice   1.20
Jesse Smith + "   7th "   1.06 1/4
William D. Trip + 1 hog 8th choice   1.20
Abraham Miller + one grind stone   .78
Thos Fitzwater + one seed hog one ton hay 2.50
George Ramsey + One sow   1.87 1/2
William D. Trip + 1 grubbing hoe   1.40
Joshua Cox   1 Hay fork   . 30 1/2
James Comb + 1 dung fork   37 1/2
John Ramedy + lott of wheat at .51 etz 3 p"
Bushel mo---half
George Ramsey + one rake .06 1/4
William D. Trip + first choie 2 sheep 4. 30
"   + 2nd " 4. 10
"   + 3rd " 3.10
Edward Johnston+ 4th "   3.10
Archibald Laferty+ 5th " 2.60
:   + last 1   1.46
George Ramsey + 5 acres of corn more or less

George Ramsey $13.00 26.00
Samuel Opdihu + 12 rows of potatoes 3.75
Timothy Buratt + 14 row of potatoes 3.87 1/2
Widow + 4 bags of potaotes 1.00
Joseph James + 1 kettle 2.50
$66.61 1/2
Widow + one white cow 8. 37 1/2
Widow + one red & white cow 8.25
Edward C. Johnson + red & white cheifer 10.00
James Comb + one harrow 2. 60
Joseph James + one farie ? . 75
Benjamin Painter + one brown steer 3.25
Charles Loper + one red steer 4.00
Widow + 12 geese & gander 1.60
Joseph James + one hog .62 1/2
James Comb + one red & white heifer 1.25
James Conb + one red bull calf 1.25

" + one claf 1. 01
Widow + upwards of 200 feet of boards.
26 ft hundred 200 ft .52
John Ramsey + 1 heifer 5.00
Hiram Parant + 1 brindle steer 6.00 1/4
Elsey McKinney + to one shovel .50
$54.54 1/4
First page 9.09 1/4
Second page 35.26
Third page 66. 61 1/2
$165.94
There is $57. 80 Ctg for the wheat carried under to
amount to sale 113 bushels V 20 pound 457.80
$223. 74
          5.25
Total amount of sale on the 20th Sept, $228,99
John Emmry & Hammond Eveland Administrators

Else McKinney 2 ton of hay at $26.24 per ton 5.25
which was not added in the amount till it was cast up & aferwards added
A. Miller 1.50
  .18 3/4
  .78
$ 2. 46 3/4

Debt & notes of long standing , notes given by Jacob McKinney and paid and taken up by William McKinny,
deceased. The said Jacob it is not known where he is and supposed to be in desperate circumstances.
Note given to Henry Hashiman by Jacob McKinny. Dated 9th of November 1816 for the sum of$28.00
A note payable four months after date to Joseph Petty Dated 2 Aug, 1816 65.00
$158.00
It is supposed that these notes never will be collected.
Due from John Ramsey to the Estate $25.00

The widow to have 7 acres of corn on the west end of the field. One beef cow.
The widow to have one hundred bushels of wheat; the small potato patch and 12 rows in the other patch the long
way.

More About WILLIAM BARKLEY:
Burial: Old Cavalry Cemetery, Clermont Co., Ohio east of Felicity

More About REBECCA NEWKIRK:
Burial: Old Cavalry Cemetery, Clermont Co., Ohio east of Felicity

Children of WILLIAM BARKLEY and REBECCA NEWKIRK are:

12.　　i.　JAMES M.⁵ BARKLEY, b. December 06, 1795, Pennsylvania; d. November 01, 1830, Washington Township, Clermont County, Ohio.

13.　　ii.　HENRY BARKLEY, b. December 30, 1797, Kentucky; d. February 24, 1859, Near Laurel, Clermont County, Ohio.

　　　iii.　JOHN BARKLEY, b. November 30, 1801, Washington Township, Clermont County, Ohio; d. February 20, 1838, Washington Township, Clermont County, Ohio; m. MARGARET P. BUCHANAN, February 16, 1827, Washington Township, Clermont County, Ohio; b. 1804; d. 1881.

　　　　Notes for JOHN BARKLEY:
　　　　Deed Book F 2 page 269. 16 January 1833: John Morford and wife Susanna of Clermont Co., Ohio sold to John Barkley of Clermont Co., Ohio. For two hundred sixty four dollars, all that certain tract or parcel of land situated in Clermont Co., Ohio, on the waters of Bear Creek . . . also corner to Morgan Neville . . . containing forty four acres of land be the same more or less. Recorded 16 January 1833.

　　　　Deed Book 02 38 page 155. Robert Fee, John Hall, John G. Buchanon, John Barkley and his wife Margaret, William P. Daughters and Hannah his wife, and Alexander Buchanan and Lamira his wife, all of the county of Clermont, Ohio, sold to Squire Frazee of Clermont Co., Ohio, for the sum of two hundred dollars paid by Squire Frazee. . . . containing 37 1/2 acres more or less. William D. Buchanan, minor heir. Recorded October 4, 1837.

　　　　Notes for MARGARET P. BUCHANAN:
　　　　Margaret was appointed guardian of Samuel G. Barkley. Bond $400, John G. Buchanan Surety.

　　　　More About MARGARET P. BUCHANAN:
　　　　Burial: Old Cavalry Cemetery, Clermont Co., Ohio east of Felicity

14.　　iv.　JOSEPH BARKLEY, b. 1812; d. December 08, 1879, Washington Township, Clermont County, Ohio.

　　　v.　KATHERINE BARKLEY, b. May 01, 1808, Clermont County, OH; d. July 02, 1866; m. JOHN P. MCKINNEY, December 17, 1829, Clermont County, Ohio.

15.　　vi.　MARY B. "POLLY" BARKLEY, b. 1824; d. 1903.

Generation No. 5

8. HUGH⁵ BARKLEY *(JOSEPH⁴, GEORGE³, JOHN² BARCLAY, DAVID BARCLAY OF¹ URIE)* was born 1794 in Washington County, Pennsylvania, and died 1860 in Effingham, Illinois. He married (1) RUTH LAYCOCK August 17, 1815 in Clermont County, Ohio. She was born 1804, and died November 1835. He married (2) KEZIAH DONHAM July 15, 1826 in Clermont County, Ohio. She was born 1805 in Clermont County, OH, and died March 08, 1851.

Children of HUGH BARKLEY and RUTH LAYCOCK are:

　　　i.　ANNE⁶ BARKLEY, b. 1816; m. JAMES HOUSTON, December 24, 1833; b. 1804.

16.　　ii.　MARTHA BARKLEY, b. December 20, 1818; d. March 17, 1863, Murfreesboro, Rutherford Co., Tennessee.

　　　iii.　ISAAC BARKLEY, b. 1820.

　　　　Notes for ISAAC BARKLEY:
　　　　"History of Clermont and Brown Counties, Ohio, page 81: On the proposed road in Washington Township beginning near Jacob Fisher's where a road from the State road ends, passing by John Flack's plantation, through Henry Cuppy's land and Thompson Gates, thence to "Gilbert's horse mill," thence to intersect Manning's and Minor's road, thence with said road to intersect the State road between William Watson's and the "Widow Harmon," William Thompson, David Smith and Peter McClain were chosen viewers, and Joseph Jackson surveyor. On the petition to turn the road leading from the "Middle Fork of Bullskin," the viewers were William S. Jump, David Miller and Isaac Barkley."

17.   iv.   NATHAN BARKLEY, b. 1821, Clermont County, OH; d. April 27, 1865, Memphis, Tennessee.

         v.   MARGARET BARKLEY, b. 1821.

Children of HUGH BARKLEY and KEZIAH DONHAM are:

         vi.   NANCY[6] BARKLEY, b. 1827.

18.   vii.   ELIZABETH M. BARKLEY, b. December 19, 1830, New Hope, Brown County, Ohio; d. February 1903, Monroe Twp., Clermont County, Ohio.

19.   viii.   FRANKLIN BARKLEY, b. 1834.

         ix.   JOHN W. BARKLEY, b. 1839.

20.   x.   ENOCH PERRY BARKLEY, b. January 03, 1841; d. May 25, 1912, Oklahoma.

9. GEORGE[5] BARKLEY *(JOSEPH[4], GEORGE[3], JOHN[2] BARCLAY, DAVID BARCLAY OF[1] URIE)* was born April 12, 1795 in Virginia, and died March 20, 1864 in Effingham, Illinois. He married FRANCES M. FIELD January 15, 1828 in Bracken, Kentucky.

Children of GEORGE BARKLEY and FRANCES FIELD are:

21.   i.   GEORGE[6] BARKLEY, b. January 15, 1818, Washington County, Pennsylvania; d. March 05, 1857, Kentucky.

         ii.   JOSEPH BARKLEY, b. 1832, Kentucky.

         iii.   JOHN BARKLEY, b. 1835, Kentucky; m. ELIZABETH SNEARLY, November 07, 1867.

22.   iv.   EMILY BARKLEY, b. 1837, Kentucky.

         v.   HENRY BARKLEY, b. 1842; m. LENORA BARRON, October 17, 1868.

         vi.   JAMES ALFRED BARKLEY, b. 1845, Illinois; m. JULIA A. CLARKE, May 01, 1870, Effingham County, Illinois.

10. ANDREW[5] BARKLEY *(JOSEPH[4], GEORGE[3], JOHN[2] BARCLAY, DAVID BARCLAY OF[1] URIE)* was born November 14, 1799 in Pennsylvania, and died July 31, 1879 in Symes, Edgar County, Illinois. He married ELIZABETH AVA MERVILLE December 09, 1826 in Brown County, Ohio. She was born 1797 in Butler County, Kentucky, and died April 02, 1879 in Symes, Edgar County, Illinois.

Children of ANDREW BARKLEY and ELIZABETH MERVILLE are:

         i.   AMANDA[6] BARKLEY, b. 1829.

23.   ii.   GEORGE WASHINGTON BARKLEY, b. January 1837, Illinois; d. 1900, Edgar, Illinois.

         iii.   DANIEL B. BARKLEY, b. 1841.

11. JOHN B.[5] BARKLEY *(JOSEPH[4], GEORGE[3], JOHN[2] BARCLAY, DAVID BARCLAY OF[1] URIE)* was born July 24, 1815 in Clermont County, OH, and died October 31, 1931 in Mayhill, Otero, New Mexico. He married SARAH CLARK February 22, 1844 in Edgar County, Illinois, daughter of SAMUEL CLARK. She was born 1821 in Clermont County, OH, and died 1864 in Effingham, Illinois.

Children of JOHN BARKLEY and SARAH CLARK are:

24.   i.   JOSEPH GEORGE[6] BARKLEY, b. December 18, 1845, Clarke County, Illinois; d. March 01, 1888, Prairie City, Grant County, Oregon.

25.   ii.   SAMUEL P. BARKLEY, b. September 27, 1848, Edgar, Illinois; d. Eureka Springs, Arkansas.

         iii.   ELIZABETH J. BARKLEY, b. July 1850, Edgar, Illinois.

26.   iv.   GEORGE W. BARKLEY, b. December 25, 1852, Effingham, Illinois; d. October 21, 1931, Mayhill, Otero, New Mexico.

27.   v.   JOHN WILLIAM BARKLEY, b. May 12, 1854, Effingham, Illinois; d. January 30, 1921, Carollton, Carroll County, Arkansas.

         vi.   MARTHA F. BARKLEY, b. November 22, 1856.

28.   vii.   SARAH ELLEN BARKLEY, b. April 10, 1859, Effingham, Illinois; d. May 08, 1933, Otero, New Mexico.

         viii.   THOMAS J. BARKLEY, b. 1864.

12. JAMES M.[5] BARKLEY *(WILLIAM[4], GEORGE[3], JOHN[2] BARCLAY, DAVID BARCLAY OF[1] URIE)* was born December 06, 1795 in Pennsylvania, and died November 01, 1830 in Washington Township, Clermont County, Ohio. He married ELIZABETH CARTER April 14, 1819 in Ohio. She was born July 09, 1801 in Bracken County, Kentucky, and died October 20, 1878 in Clermont County, OH.

Children of JAMES BARKLEY and ELIZABETH CARTER are:

29.   i.   WILLIAM G.⁶ BARKLEY, b. May 27, 1820, Clermont County, OH; d. 1900.
30.   ii.   CATHERINE ELLA BARKLEY, b. January 03, 1822, Clermont County, OH; d. October 08, 1884, Clermont County, OH.
31.   iii. PERRY HENRY BARKLEY, b. April 30, 1824, Ohio; d. April 16, 1886, New Richmond, Clermont, County, Ohio.
       iv.   REBECCA EMELINE BARKLEY, b. April 09, 1826, Clermont County, OH; d. 1897; m. JAMES CORBIN, January 01, 1846, Clermont County, Ohio; b. 1817; d. 1891.

             Notes for REBECCA EMELINE BARKLEY:
             Married by A. L. McLahahlin, M.M.E.C.

32.   v.   HENRY CARTER BARKLEY, b. December 02, 1827, Clermont County, OH; d. November 12, 1892, Clermont County, OH.
33.   vi.   JAMES M. BARKLEY, b. January 24, 1831, Clermont County, OH; d. September 04, 1851, Clermont County, OH.

13. HENRY⁵ BARKLEY *(WILLIAM⁴, GEORGE³, JOHN² BARCLAY, DAVID BARCLAY OF¹ URIE)* was born December 30, 1797 in Kentucky, and died February 24, 1859 in Near Laurel, Clermont County, Ohio. He married SARAH (SALLY) BROWN December 08, 1829 in Clermont County, Ohio. She died November 14, 1849.

Notes for HENRY BARKLEY:
He was 61 years, 24 days at the time of his death. In 1837 some of the owners of houses and shops in New Richmond were Bennett N. Barber and Henry Barkley.

Deed Book T 18 page 261, March 18, 1826. Hugh Barckley (sic) sold to Henry Barckley (sic) for $225 dollars land in Clermont County, Ohio. A tract entered in the name of John Woodford No. 4126, bounded and beginning at two beeches and a white oak, . . . to a stone by a plum and beech corner to Nicholas Corbin, . . . witnessed by a beech and red oak corner to George Barckley (sic) . . . containing fifty acres. Sealed March 18, 1826.

Deed Book C 27 page 84, July 30, 1830. Henry Barkley of Clermont County, Ohio, was appointed by the Court of Common Pleas concerning the will of David Brown, John and Elizabeth Corbin, 2nd September 1824, filed in the clerk's office. David and Elizabeth Brown, having made and duly published his last Will and Testament, leaving Margaret Brown, his wife, the sole Executrix of said Will, the said Elizabeth J. Corbin, Sarah Brown, Mary Brown, Enoch Brown legal heirs, September 7, 1818. Money from sale should be equally divided between his four children, Elizabeth J, Sarah, Mary and Enoch and lands directed to be sold after the death of said Executrix, as by reference to said will. Margaret Brown sold on the 24th of May 1829, departed this life interstate. David Brown had seized for of 140 acres of land in Clermont County, part of entry entered in the name of John McDougal. Henry Barkley sold 140 acres at a sale at a hundred thirty three dollars to John Corbin. Recorded 7 December, 1830.

Henry Barkley Will:
Know all men by these presents, that I, Henry Barkley of the County of Clermont and State of Ohio, being now of sound mind and memory, in view of the uncertainty of life, do by these presence declare this to be my last Will and Testament for the benefit and use of my children: Maria J. Barkley, Elizabeth R. Barkley, John L. Barkley, William S. Barkley and George H. B. Barkley.
1st: To my oldest son John L. Barkley, I give and bequeath the home farm upon which I now live, consisting of two hundred acres more or less and situated in Monroe Township, County and State aforesaid, he the said John IL Barkley, to pay my executors the sum of fifteen hundred and fourteen dollars in six equal payments (of one, two, three, four, five and six years) without interest.
2nd: To my son William S. Barkley, I give and bequeath the sum of five thousand dollars in cash to be paid to him by my Executors from the proceeds of my estate.
3rd: To my youngest son George H. B. Barkley, I give and bequeath the land and appurations known as the Davis farm, consisting of one hundred and thirty acres more or less, situated in Monroe Twp., County and State

aforesaid and the further sum of ten hundred and twenty dollars in cash to be paid to him by my Executors from the proceeds of my estate.

4th: To my eldest daughter Maria J. Barkley, I give and bequeath the sum of four thousand dollars in cash to be paid to him by my Executors.

5th: To my next daughter Elizabeth R. Barkley, I give and bequeath the sum of four thousand dollars in cash to be paid to him by my Executors.

6th: My meadow farm, containing fifty acres situated in Monroe Township, County and State aforesaid and which has been estimated in my assets, I wish sold by my Executors as soon as can be done to advantage and proceeds applied to the payment of the several bequests as above expressed.

7th: My interest in the home farm at the disposal of Joseph Barkley, Executor, by the will of my father William Barkley deceased and subject to the life of my mother Rebecca Barkley, situated in Washington Township, County of Clermont and State of Ohio, when sold divided between my sons, John L. Barkley, William S. Barkley, and George H. B. Barkley.

8th: My chattel property to the amount of one thousand dollars to be held in common by my heirs so long as they continue to live together. Afterwards to be sold to said amount by my Executors and proceeds applied to the payment of bequests as herein expressed.

9th: In the division or sale of my chattle out side of the house, I give and bequeath to my son John L. Barkley a team consisting of three horses and one wagon. As such other farming implements as will be necessary to carry on the work of the farm, provided that the said John L. Barkley continues to live on said house and farm and provides and shares in common during his minority with the balance of my heirs.

10th: The balance of my chattle property, consisting of house hold goods, to be distributed as near equal as possible without sale to my heirs as herein mentioned and I hereby constitute Elizabeth J. Corbin and Polly Robbison, my agents to carry this bequest into execution.

11th: To my son William S. Barkley, I give and bequeath one horse, saddle and bridal, which is to remain upon the farm for his use and benefit, provided he let said horse remain upon the farm for common use during his minority.

12th: It is understood that during the minority of my oldest son, John L. Barkley, that the family are to live together and their said living is to be made in common from the proceeds of the Home farm and other lands and it is further understood that the said John L. Barkley in consequence of the provisions made to him in this my will, that Maria J. Barkley and Elizabeth R. Barkley, so long as they continue unmarried and William S. Barkley and George H. B. Barkley, during their minority are to have a home with the said John L. Barkley, without charge, they to do and perform such labor as is common in families and the said William S. Barkley and George H. B. Barkley are to have the privilege of attending school at their own expense.

And I hereby appoint Perry J. Barkley and Thos. C. Gowdy as my Executors to carry this my last Will and Testament in to effect, done this Tenth day of February, year of our Lord, A.D. 1859. As witnessed by my hand and seal. Henry Barkley. Witnesses: Silar F. Robbins and Hezikiah Lindsey.

Codicil Made to the foregoing Will made this 18th day of February, A.D., 1859:

1st: It is my wish that all the moneys, notes, interest on notes and other evidence of debt should remain as they now exist unless my Executors should consider it in danger of loss, the accumulation interest to be reinvested unless wanted for the support of my heirs under the will.

2nd: I give and bequeath to my daughter, Maria J. Barkley, one Piano, which is now in the possession of my family.

3rd: To my daughter, Elizabeth R. Barkley, I give and bequeath, out of my moneys out of any not hither to approprated the sum of one hundred dollars in lieu of her share in the piano, which I have this day willed to my daughter Maria J. Barkley.

4th: And I hereby appoint my brother-in-law Ed (?) Brown as guardian under this my last Will and Testament for my young son George H. B. Barkley.

5th: It is to be understood that my farming implements, subject to the use of John L. Barkley as necessary to carrry on the work of the farm shall not exceed the sum of one hundred dollars, the grease belonging to the horses and wagon bequeathed to him to be considered as a part of the team.

6th: Out of any proceeds that may arise from any surplus of my estate, after the payment of all legacies under this Will and costs of Executorship, Probate expenses, I give and bequeath to my son William S. Barkley the sum of five hundred dollars, over and above that already bequeathed and any remainder to be divided equally between my heirs. As witnessed my hand and seal day and date above written. Henry Barkley. Same witnesses proved March 16, 1859,

Notes for SARAH (SALLY) BROWN:
Also calle Sally Bell Brown. She was 37 years old when she died.

More About SARAH (SALLY) BROWN:
Burial: Laurel Cemetery, Clermont County, Ohio

Children of HENRY BARKLEY and SARAH BROWN are:
    i.   MARIA J.[6] BARKLEY.
    ii.   ELIZABETH R. BARKLEY.
    iii.   JOHN L. BARKLEY, b. 1840; d. 1894.

        Notes for JOHN L. BARKLEY:
        "History of Clermont and Brown Counties, 1878." John L. Barkley was Treasurer for the fair (The exhibition this season was unusually interesting from the grand display of fruits and vegetables and stock, of which of the latter many blooded horses and imported stock of cattle were from a distance and some from Kentucky. The increasing shade and foliage of the growing trees added much to the comfort of those in attendance). 1879 - John L. Barkley was again Treasurer.

    iv.   WILLIAM S. BARKLEY.
    v.   GEORGE H. B. BARKLEY.
    vi.   MARGARET GEORGE ANN BARKLEY.
    vii.   DAVID WILLIAM BARKLEY, b. 1832, Laurel, Hocking County, Ohio; d. October 23, 1834.

        More About DAVID WILLIAM BARKLEY:
        Burial: Laurel Cemetery, Clermont County, Ohio

14. JOSEPH[5] BARKLEY *(WILLIAM[4], GEORGE[3], JOHN[2] BARCLAY, DAVID BARCLAY OF[1] URIE)* was born 1812, and died December 08, 1879 in Washington Township, Clermont County, Ohio. He married FLORENCE/FLORELLA C. WOOD October 06, 1833 in Clermont County, Ohio. She was born 1811, and died March 18, 1871.

Notes for JOSEPH BARKLEY:
Deed Book Q2 40 page 196. 12 November 1838. William H. Wood of Clermont County, Ohio sold to Joseph Barkley for two hundred and thirty three dollars, land in Clermont County, Ohio. A certain undivided tract of land containing 100 acres in the Township of Washington, Clermont County, Ohio. On the waters of Bear Creek, a part of a survey entered in William Smith's name No. 866. Sealed 12 November, 1838. Recorded 22 November, 1838.

Will to-wit: November 24th, 1870
"At home, in Washington Township, Clermont County, Ohio. I, Joseph Barkley, make this my last Will and Bequest. Being of sound mind etc., my wife Florella Barkley shall have full possession and control of my land and chattles during her life for her own use and benefit, subject to these restrictions, to sell such personal property as she may see cause and settle my indebtedness, the balance to be at her disposal, at my wife's death the estate is to be equally divided between my legal heirs at law, subject only to this restriction, that William Barl\kley, my oldest son has had his bed and board at home for at least five years, I claim an offset against him in the sum of five hundred dollars, and his share shall be less than the balance of the heirs (in the said sum of five hundred dollars).
In witness whereof I hereunto set my and and seal this November 24th, 1870. Joseph Barkley {Seal} Proved 1870.
We, the undersigned residents of Washington Township, Clermont County, having read the contents of the above Will, witnessed the signing of the same by the Testator. Attest: James Frisler and Nathan Cottell."

OLD CALVARY CEMETERY: These are all on stone: carved on all sides of the stone:
Joseph Barkley, died December 8, 1878, 87 years
Florella Barkley, His Wife, died March 18 1871, aged 60 years
Liaaie S. Barkley, dau. of J. & F. Barkley, died December 18, 1876, 29 years

Joseph H. Barkley, son of J. & F. Barkley, died March 17, 1871, 25 years
Bell R. Barkley, dau. of J. & F. Barkley, died July 3, 1872, aged 21 years
W. G. Barkley, b. June 18, 1838, died September 27, 1870

Other stones:
Margaret Barkley, wife of John Barkley, b. December 15, 1804, d. March 2, 1881
Sarah R. Barkley, dau. of Joseph & Florella Barkley, died June 28, 1845 in 10th year
John Barkley, died February 20, 1830 in 38th year
George Barkley, died April 21, 1837 in 71st year, Revolutionary Soldier

More About JOSEPH BARKLEY:
Burial: Old Cavalry Cemetery, Clermont Co., Ohio east of Felicity

Children of JOSEPH BARKLEY and FLORENCE/FLORELLA WOOD are:
     i.   BARKLEY[6] BARKLEY.
     ii.   ELIZABETH S. BARKLEY.
     iii.   JAMES H. BARKLEY.
     iv.   JOSEPH HENRY LOUIS BARKLEY, m. MARY ELIZABETH BARBER; b. April 01, 1862, Ohio; d. July 01, 1930, Archie, Cass County, MO.

          More About MARY ELIZABETH BARBER:
          Burial: Mt. Olivet Cemetery SE of Adrian, Missouri, Bates County

     v.   LAURA FLORILLA BARKLEY.
     vi.   REBECCA BARKLEY.
34.   vii.   MARY JANE BARKLEY, b. 1835, Clermont County, OH.
     viii.   WILLIAM G. BARKLEY, b. June 1838.
     ix.   MARGARET SALINA BARKLEY, b. 1840.
35.   x.   LUCY MAXWELL BARKLEY, b. September 15, 1841, Washington Township, Clermont, Ohio; d. July 08, 1908, Clermont County, OH.
     xi.   LOUISA A. BARKLEY, b. 1842.
     xii.   JOHN C. BARKLEY.

15. MARY B. "POLLY"[5] BARKLEY *(WILLIAM[4], GEORGE[3], JOHN[2] BARCLAY, DAVID BARCLAY OF[1] URIE)* was born 1824, and died 1903. She married JOHN H. WOOD January 28, 1838 in Clermont County, Ohio. He was born 1823 in Clermont County, OH.

Notes for MARY B. "POLLY" BARKLEY:
Rebecca Newkirk Barkley was living with Mary and John H. Wood in 1850. Rebecca was 76 years old born in Pennsylvania.

Children of MARY BARKLEY and JOHN WOOD are:
     i.   FLORILLA[6] WOOD, b. 1840.
     ii.   JOSEPH H. WOOD, b. 1842.

Generation No. 6

16. MARTHA[6] BARKLEY *(HUGH[5], JOSEPH[4], GEORGE[3], JOHN[2] BARCLAY, DAVID BARCLAY OF[1] URIE)* was born December 20, 1818, and died March 17, 1863 in Murfreesboro, Rutherford Co., Tennessee. She married JOHN ABRAHAM July 27, 1836 in Clermont County, Ohio. He was born December 28, 1766 in Chester, Chester County, Pennsylvania, and died November 14, 1851 in Clermont County, OH.

Children of MARTHA BARKLEY and JOHN ABRAHAM are:
     i.   KIDS[7] ABRAHAM.
     ii.   WILLIAM MILTON ABRAHAM, b. July 26, 1842, Bethal, Clermont County, Ohio; d. June 28, 1914, Watson, Effingham, Illinois; m. ELIZA RALSTON WAYNE; b. June 21, 1842, Shelbyville, Shelby County, Kentucky;

d. January 27, 1927, Effingham, Illinois.
iii. ZELLA MARCELLA ABRAHAM, b. 1848.
iv. OLIVIA FRANCES ABRAHAM, b. September 10, 1848.
v. ZILLAH ZELIAH ABRAHAM, b. October 03, 1851.

17. NATHAN[6] BARKLEY *(HUGH[5], JOSEPH[4], GEORGE[3], JOHN[2] BARCLAY, DAVID BARCLAY OF[1] URIE)* was born 1821 in Clermont County, OH, and died April 27, 1865 in Memphis, Tennessee. He married SARAH ANN DENNISTON October 03, 1847 in Clermont County, Ohio. She was born July 17, 1829 in Clermont County, OH, and died January 08, 1914 in Dayton, Montgomery, Ohio.

Children of NATHAN BARKLEY and SARAH DENNISTON are:
i. FANCIS M.[7] BARKLEY, b. 1849.
ii. LORISSA B. BARKLEY, b. 1851.
iii. LARISA BELLE BARKLEY, b. 1851; d. 1941; m. FRANCIS LAFAYETTE MCDONALD, April 04, 1885, Greene, Ohio; b. September 19, 1846, Clermont County, OH; d. April 13, 1911, Darke, Ohio.
iv. GEORGIANNA BARKLEY, b. 1855.
v. CHARLES A. BARKLEY, b. 1858.
vi. LETITIA BARKLEY, b. 1861.

18. ELIZABETH M.[6] BARKLEY *(HUGH[5], JOSEPH[4], GEORGE[3], JOHN[2] BARCLAY, DAVID BARCLAY OF[1] URIE)* was born December 19, 1830 in New Hope, Brown County, Ohio, and died February 1903 in Monroe Twp., Clermont County, Ohio. She married LEWIS CARNES May 29, 1851 in Clermont County, Ohio, son of JOSIAH CARNES and PATIENCE MARSH. He was born July 18, 1799 in Washington, Mason County, Kentucky, and died May 08, 1884 in Monroe Twp., Clermont County, Ohio.

Children of ELIZABETH BARKLEY and LEWIS CARNES are:
i. JESSE LUTHER[7] CARNES, b. 1852; d. September 01, 1868.
ii. CHARLES E. CARNES, b. 1854; d. 1912, Monroe Twp., Clermont County, Ohio; m. EMMA BOYS.
iii. GRACE CARNES.
iv. ABIGAIL CARNES.
v. ARTHUR L. CARNES, b. October 18, 1856; m. FLORENCE DONALDSON.

19. FRANKLIN[6] BARKLEY *(HUGH[5], JOSEPH[4], GEORGE[3], JOHN[2] BARCLAY, DAVID BARCLAY OF[1] URIE)* was born 1834. He married MALINDA. She was born 1844 in Ohio.

Children of FRANKLIN BARKLEY and MALINDA are:
i. SARAH[7] BARKLEY, b. 1863, Gentry, Missouri.
ii. FRANK BARKLEY, b. 1869, Gentry, Missouri.

20. ENOCH PERRY[6] BARKLEY *(HUGH[5], JOSEPH[4], GEORGE[3], JOHN[2] BARCLAY, DAVID BARCLAY OF[1] URIE)* was born January 03, 1841, and died May 25, 1912 in Oklahoma. He married ISABELLA GRANTHAM. She was born April 02, 1841 in Illinois, and died March 08, 1916 in Franklin Corners, California.

Children of ENOCH BARKLEY and ISABELLA GRANTHAM are:
i. JOHN ELBERT[7] BARKLEY, b. November 06, 1863, Gentry, Missouri; m. ABBIE FOSTER, October 26, 1886.
ii. LUTHER ELLSWORTH BARKLEY, b. November 13, 1865, Gentry, Missouri; d. May 22, 1940, Blackwell, Oklahoma; m. LAURA BELLE MCALLISTER, July 15, 1887, Ellsworth, Kansas; b. July 04, 1867, Monroe, Iowa; d. October 27, 1939, Pampa Gray, Texas.
iii. WILLIAM EDGAR BARKLEY, b. November 28, 1868.
iv. CHARLEY WALTER BARKLEY, b. July 16, 1871, Gentry, Missouri; d. April 24, 1926; m. (1) ETHEL SMITH, October 22, 1899; d. February 20, 1910; m. (2) ELLA MCLAUGHLIN, July 19, 1905.
v. OLLIE EUPHEMIA BARKLEY, b. February 21, 1875; d. May 17, 1890.
vi. LAURA DALE BARKLEY, b. June 17, 1877, Albany, Missouri; d. September 14, 1954, Alva, Oklahoma; m. ELLIS U. ANDERSON, September 15, 1895; b. December 15, 1872, Alva, Oklahoma; d. October 25, 1958, Alva, Oklahoma.
vii. ILA MAUDE BARKLEY, b. April 05, 1879, Kansas; m. ADRIN S. FOSTER, July 10, 1898, Kansas.

viii.   BERTHA BELL BARKLEY, b. May 11, 1884; m. BERT HILL; b. Abt. 1883, Kansas.

21. GEORGE[6] BARKLEY *(GEORGE[5], JOSEPH[4], GEORGE[3], JOHN[2] BARCLAY, DAVID BARCLAY OF[1] URIE)* was born January 15, 1818 in Washington County, Pennsylvania, and died March 05, 1857 in Kentucky. He married SARAH WELCH March 15, 1842 in Edgar County, Illinois. She was born 1820, and died 1889.

Children of GEORGE BARKLEY and SARAH WELCH are:
    i.   ANN M.[7] BARKLEY, b. 1845, Edgar, Illinois; d. 1860.
    ii.   WILLIAM N. BARKLEY, b. 1848, Edgar, Illinois; d. 1870; m. NANCY ELIZABETH BANTA; b. August 25, 1855, Illinois.

22. EMILY[6] BARKLEY *(GEORGE[5], JOSEPH[4], GEORGE[3], JOHN[2] BARCLAY, DAVID BARCLAY OF[1] URIE)* was born 1837 in Kentucky. She married MR. MCCANN June 21, 1857 in Effingham County, Illinois.

Child of EMILY BARKLEY and MR. MCCANN is:
    i.   CLARA[7] MCCANN.

23. GEORGE WASHINGTON[6] BARKLEY *(ANDREW[5], JOSEPH[4], GEORGE[3], JOHN[2] BARCLAY, DAVID BARCLAY OF[1] URIE)* was born January 1837 in Illinois, and died 1900 in Edgar, Illinois. He married NANCY WHEETEN March 11, 1862 in Illinois. She was born 1834 in Illinois.

Child of GEORGE BARKLEY and NANCY WHEETEN is:
36.   i.   WILLIAM HENRY[7] BARKLEY, b. 1858, Ohio; d. 1927, Texas.

24. JOSEPH GEORGE[6] BARKLEY *(JOHN B.[5], JOSEPH[4], GEORGE[3], JOHN[2] BARCLAY, DAVID BARCLAY OF[1] URIE)* was born December 18, 1845 in Clarke County, Illinois, and died March 01, 1888 in Prairie City, Grant County, Oregon. He married JOSEPHINE DRUCILLA METZGER March 21, 1857 in Clark County, Illinois. She was born November 09, 1842 in Illinois, and died September 24, 1921 in Newberg, Yamill, Oregon.

Children of JOSEPH BARKLEY and JOSEPHINE METZGER are:
    i.   SARAH JANE[7] BARKLEY, b. February 07, 1865; m. HYLE ACE HYDE, February 07, 1887, Prairie City, Grant, Oregon; b. March 28, 1841, Westerville Franklin, New York; d. November 13, 1917, Newberg, Yamill, Oregon.
    ii.   ROSA E. BARKLEY, b. Abt. 1867; m. BRACKETT JOHNSON, December 23, 1888, Grant, Oregon; b. 1847, Missouri.
    iii.   LENORA E. BARKLEY, b. 1868; m. W. W. ARMSTRONG, June 18, 1887, Grant, Oregon; b. September 09, 1830; d. September 24, 1904, Canon City, Grant, Oregon.
    iv.   FLORA C. BARKLEY, b. December 31, 1870; m. (1) LUDWIG FREIDRICH NIERMANN, 1890; m. (2) LEWISNIERMANN, November 02, 1890, Grant, Oregon; m. (3) DAVID ANDREW MILLER, October 29, 1905; b. Abt. 1870.
    v.   CHARLES ALEXANDER BARKLEY, b. February 1875.
    vi.   JOHN W. BARKLEY, b. Abt. 1877.
    vii.   SILAS BARKLEY, b. November 27, 1878.
    viii. PAUL BARKLEY, b. November 27, 1878, Montague, Texas; d. Abt. 1925, Montana.
    ix.   WILLIAM ALFRED BARKLEY, b. January 09, 1881, Texas; d. April 08, 1971, Pendleton, Umatilla, Oregon.
    x.   VIDA MAY BARKLEY, b. October 19, 1884, Oregon; d. October 28, 1897, Prairie City, Grant County, Oregon.

25. SAMUEL P.[6] BARKLEY *(JOHN B.[5], JOSEPH[4], GEORGE[3], JOHN[2] BARCLAY, DAVID BARCLAY OF[1] URIE)* was born September 27, 1848 in Edgar, Illinois, and died in Eureka Springs, Arkansas. He married MARY LOUISE WALKEN.

Children of SAMUEL BARKLEY and MARY WALKEN are:
    i.   LYDIA LILLIE[7] BARKLEY, b. 1881; m. FRANK DRAKE, February 11, 1902, Paris, Edgar County, Illinois.
    ii.   MADIE BARKLEY, b. September 22, 1892.

26. GEORGE W.[6] BARKLEY *(JOHN B.[5], JOSEPH[4], GEORGE[3], JOHN[2] BARCLAY, DAVID BARCLAY OF[1] URIE)* was born December 25, 1852 in Effingham, Illinois, and died October 21, 1931 in Mayhill, Otero, New Mexico. He married ARTENSIA E. WILSON November 17, 1872 in Rusk, Texas. She was born April 10, 1852 in Rusk, Texas, and died January 11, 1929 in High Rolls, Otero, New Mexico.

Children of GEORGE BARKLEY and ARTENSIA WILSON are:
-   i.   GEORGE P.[7] BARKLEY, b. September 18, 1876, Texas; d. November 06, 1968; m. ONA COX.
-   ii. MARY ELLEN BARKLEY, b. April 13, 1878, Texas; d. July 06, 1957, Otero, New Mexico; m. JASPER N. SCOTT, 1899, New Mexico; b. September 15, 1873, Texas; d. July 12, 1951, Otero, New Mexico.
-   iii. JOHN GORDON BARKLEY, b. February 20, 1889.

27. JOHN WILLIAM[6] BARKLEY *(JOHN B.[5], JOSEPH[4], GEORGE[3], JOHN[2] BARCLAY, DAVID BARCLAY OF[1] URIE)* was born May 12, 1854 in Effingham, Illinois, and died January 30, 1921 in Carollton, Carroll County, Arkansas. He married JOHANNA E. PARSON October 21, 1877 in Bowie, Montague, Texas. She was born October 30, 1862 in Wise, Texas, and died July 07, 1931 in Duncan, Stephens, Oklahoma.

Children of JOHN BARKLEY and JOHANNA PARSON are:
-   i.   VALLIE MAE[7] BARKLEY, b. February 05, 1879, Montague, Texas; d. March 01, 1951, Stephens, Oklahoma; m. JESSE JAMES KERNS, 1906.
-   ii.   AVA LEE BARKLEY, b. May 27, 1880, Montague, Texas; d. November 12, 1918, Ephrate Grant, Washington; m. GEORGE PRUITT.
-   iii. HANSON BARKLEY, b. July 08, 1882, Montague, Texas; d. February 1968, Snyder, Scurry, Texas; m. MAUDE TURNER, 1889.
-   iv.   MARY BARKLEY, b. July 1883, Montague, Texas; d. July 1883, Montague, Texas.
-   v.   MARTHA BARKLEY, b. July 1883.
-   vi.   ALMA JANE BARKLEY, b. August 30, 1884, Montague, Texas; d. October 12, 1885, Montague, Texas.
-   vii. VIDA BELLE BARKLEY, b. August 11, 1886, Montague, Texas; d. October 07, 1890, Montague, Texas.
-   viii. AUTIE WILLIAM BARKLEY, b. September 21, 1888, Montague, Texas; d. January 01, 1919, Duncan, Stephens, Oklahoma; m. CONNIE KERNS.
-   ix.   IRBY FOREST BARKLEY, b. February 23, 1891, Montague, Texas; d. July 13, 1969, Ottawa, Franklin, Kansas; m. MIMA MILLER.
-   x.   FLEDDA JOHANNA BARKLEY, b. July 17, 1892, Snyder, Scurry, Texas; d. October 22, 1928, Lawton, Oklahoma; m. DRURY OSCAR FAIRLEY, October 01, 1911.
-   xi.   GEORGE ELMER BARKLEY, b. 1894, Snyder, Scurry, Texas; d. September 06, 1987, Meridan, Idaho; m. BESSIE RAINES.
-   xii. MILLARD ODA BARKLEY, b. March 07, 1896, Snyder, Scurry, Texas; d. November 07, 1918, France.
-   xiii. ORMA ELLEN BARKLEY, b. August 23, 1897, Snyder, Scurry, Texas; d. January 27, 1988, Chester, Major, Oklahoma; m. WESLEY BOWERS.
-   xiv. JESSIE PEARL BARKLEY, b. March 30, 1900, Snyder, Scurry, Texas; d. November 29, 1997, St. Helens, Oregon; m. ROBERT MILLARD STAPE, October 05, 1919, Carroll County, Arkansas.
-   xv.   CHARLEY BARKLEY, b. February 27, 1902, Snyder, Scurry, Texas; d. March 05, 1902, Snyder, Scurry, Texas.
-   xvi. JAMES ROY BARKLEY, b. April 15, 1903, Snyder, Scurry, Texas; d. October 20, 1957, Green Forest, Carroll County, Arkansas; m. IVA STAPE.

28. SARAH ELLEN[6] BARKLEY *(JOHN B.[5], JOSEPH[4], GEORGE[3], JOHN[2] BARCLAY, DAVID BARCLAY OF[1] URIE)* was born April 10, 1859 in Effingham, Illinois, and died May 08, 1933 in Otero, New Mexico. She married JOHN WISEMAN NATIONS April 13, 1878 in Wise, Montague City, Texas. He was born February 03, 1839 in Missouri, and died February 17, 1907.

Children of SARAH BARKLEY and JOHN NATIONS are:
-   i.   FLORA[7] NATIONS.
-   ii. NELLIE NATIONS.
-   iii. MINNIE MYRTLE NATIONS, b. February 26, 1881.
-   iv. MARY LUCRETIA NATIONS, b. November 29, 1882.
-   v.   GEORGE W. NATIONS, b. 1887.
-   vi. J. BENJAMIN NATIONS, b. September 25, 1891.

vii.   JOSEPHINE PEARL NATIONS, b. 1894.
viii. JAMES G. NATIONS, b. 1896.

29. WILLIAM G.[6] BARKLEY (*JAMES M.[5], WILLIAM[4], GEORGE[3], JOHN[2] BARCLAY, DAVID BARCLAY OF[1] URIE*) was born May 27, 1820 in Clermont County, OH, and died 1900. He married CHARLOTTE NORRIS. She was born 1827.

Children of WILLIAM BARKLEY and CHARLOTTE NORRIS are:
   i.   MELISSA J.[7] BARKLEY, b. 1844.
   ii.   MARY C. BARKLEY, b. 1850.
   iii. REBECCA ELLEN BARKLEY, b. 1852.
   iv.   WILLIAM P. BARKLEY, b. 1857.
   v.   GEORGE BARKLEY, b. 1861.

30. CATHERINE ELLA[6] BARKLEY (*JAMES M.[5], WILLIAM[4], GEORGE[3], JOHN[2] BARCLAY, DAVID BARCLAY OF[1] URIE*) was born January 03, 1822 in Clermont County, OH, and died October 08, 1884 in Clermont County, OH. She married (1) JAMES C. COOPER March 19, 1837 in Clermont County, Ohio. He was born in Clermont County, OH, and died March 06, 1869 in Clermont County, OH. She married (2) DAVID STEELMAN November 24, 1872 in Clermont County, Ohio.

More About CATHERINE ELLA BARKLEY:
Burial: Mt. Zion Cemetery, Clermont, Ohio

Children of CATHERINE BARKLEY and JAMES COOPER are:
   i.   ELIZABETH REBECCA[7] COOPER, b. April 18, 1840.
   ii.   MARY ELLEN COOPER, b. November 02, 1841.
   iii. MARIA JANE COOPER, b. February 23, 1845.
   iv.   LOUISA MALVINA COOPER, b. September 13, 1848.
   v.   WILLIAM COOPER, b. 1854.
   vi.   JAMES PERRY COOPER, b. July 14, 1861.
   vii. CHARLES COOPER, b. 1863.

31. PERRY HENRY[6] BARKLEY (*JAMES M.[5], WILLIAM[4], GEORGE[3], JOHN[2] BARCLAY, DAVID BARCLAY OF[1] URIE*) was born April 30, 1824 in Ohio, and died April 16, 1886 in New Richmond, Clermont, County, Ohio. He married MARY MAE STILLMAN September 28, 1845 in Clermont County, Ohio. She was born 1826, and died 1907 in New Richmond, Clermont County, Ohio.

Notes for PERRY HENRY BARKLEY:
Will: In the matter of the Will of Perry H. Barkley, dec'd.
This day came Joseph H. Barkley and presented to the Court an instrument of writing purporting to be the last Will and Testament of Perry H. Barkley, late of Clermont County, Ohio, deceased, and made application to admit the same to Probate, and that the Court find that due notice of the filing of said will and the application to admit the same to Probate and the Court find that due notice of the filing of said will and the application this day and that the same would be for hearing this day has been given in writing to Charles C. Barkley, minor child of said deceased, residing in Ohio, and therefore came Mary Barkley widow and Theodore W. Barkley and Hosea S. Barkley who with said Joseph H. and Charles C. Barkley are the only ones of the next of kin of said decedent who reside in Ohio and being all of lawful age in open Court waived notice and consented to the probate of said Will forthwith, and therefore came W. L. Moreton and John West the subscribing witnesses to said Will and being sworn according to law testified to the due execution of said Will . . . It is therefore, ordered that the said Will be and it is hereby admitt ed to probate and that it be recorded together with said testimony. And therefore came the said Joseph H. Barkley and Mary Barkley the executors named in said Will and in open Court, accepted said trust; and it is ordered that letters Testamentary issue to them herein and that the same be recorded . . .

Will, to -wit:
Know all men by these present that I, Perry H. Barkley, of Clermont County and state of Ohio being now of

David Barclay of Urie, Scotland

sound mind and memory in vie of the uncertain of life do by these presence declare this to be my last Will and Testament for the use and benefit of my wife Mary Barkley and my sons James W. Barkley, Joseph H. Barkley, Theodore W. Barkley, Asa T. Barkley, Hosea S. Barkley, and Charles C. Barkley as follows:

Item 1: To my wife Mary Barkley, after all my debts are paid, I give device and bequeath my home farm on whitch we now live containing one hundred and eighteen acres mor or less situate in Monroe Township, County and State above named and all that is in the house to hold and use for her suport during her natural life so long as she remains my widow my said wife to keep up the nessary repair on said farm after the same comes into her possession ut of the surplus proceds of said farm over and above her suport and the residence of said surplus she can use and dispose of as she sees proper.

Item 2: I will and direct that my executors herein after named or the survivor of them shall controle and manage all my estate both real and personal untill all my debts funeral expences and cost of administration are paid my chattel property that I may have at my death my executors can dispose of as they may think best for the interest of my estate without appraisal and to that end I hereby invest my said executors or the survivors of them with full power to sell said personal property belonging to my estate at private or public sale as in their judgment shall seem best.

Item 3: It is my wish that my son Hosea S. Barkley remain as tenant on said farm untill my debts funeral expences and cost of administration are settled and paid, he to pay usual rent or as he and my executors may agree upon but in no event is my wife Mary Barkley to be disturbed in the controle and possession of the dwelling house where we now live during her natural life or widowhood. I direct that my excutors give to my youngest son Charles C. Barkley a good business education to be paid out of the proceeds of said farm, he to have a home with his mother when not at way at school.

Item 4: During the time my executors are necessarly occupied in settling up my estate they are to received the rents of said farm and aply the proceeds first to the nessary suport of my wife Mary Barkley, second to the necessary repairs on said farm and the surplus to the payment of debts funeral expenses and cost of administration and so soon as my estate is settled up or as near as can be during my wife life then my said wife Mary Barkley is to have full controle and possession of said farm during her natural life or so long as she remains my widow.

Item 5: It is my wish that upon the death of my wife that my sons so arrange that some of them shall own the aforesaid farm if that cannot be done than it is my wish that my sons aforesaid or their heirs agree upon and make among themselves an amicable partition of said farm and household goods equally and justly amongst themselfs; in case an amicable partition of said farm from any caus cannot be agreed upon by and between my said sons or their legal representation then and in that case I hereby authorise, and impower my surviving executor to sell said farm at publict or private sale to the best advantage and to make title thereto to the purchaser by good and suficient deed and I direct him to divide the proceds of such sale equally among my said sons and their legal representataves.

Item 6: If upon the final settlement of my estate among my executor and other sons there arises any dissatifaction or dispute between my executor and other sons I direct that such matter of difference be settled by arbitration as follows, my executor to select one disinterested man my other sons to select one disinterested man and those two to select a third disinterested man and the mater of dispute or difference shall be submitte to these three men so selected and their award shall be final among all concerned, if any one or more of my said sons refuse to abide by the finding and dicession of these three men so selected and take the matter to court or go to law about any matte concerning my estate sutch of my sons as refuse to arbitrate differences do herein directed or that shall go to law with his brothers or my executor touching any matter of my estate sutch son or sons shall forfeit all clame to any part of my estate and shall have no interest in or under any provision of this my Will.

Item 7: I hereby apoint my wife Mary Barkley and my son Joseph H. Barkley my executors with full power to carry out the provisions of this my Will I do not desire that my executors or eather or them be required to give bond or to incur any other costs than a probate of this my Will. I direct that no inventory or apraisement of my estate be maid. I wish my executor Joseph H. Barkley to keep an itemized account of the executors expences and time employed in settling my estate and I wish my other sons to allow the amount if fair and just and if they decline to do so than I wish the probate court to allow my executors a just compensation for services that they or eather or them may have rendered in the settlement of my estate.

In witness whereof I have hereunto set my hand and seal this the 30th day of April 1883.

Perry H. Barkley {seal}

The foregoing instrument consisting of one and one half sheet subscribed by Perry H. Barkley the testator in the presence of us and of each of us and was at the same time declared by him to be his last Will and Testament and we at his request sign our names hereto as attesting witnesses in his presence and in each others prescence.

W. L. Moreton and John West

David Barclay of Urie, Scotland

Probated: September 7, 1886, Clermont, Ohio [Ohio Wills, Vol. N-O, 1881-1887]

More About MARY MAE STILLMAN:
Burial: Mount Zion Cemetery, New Richmond, Clermont County, Ohio

Children of PERRY BARKLEY and MARY STILLMAN are:

i. DAVID H.[7] BARKLEY, b. 1847.
ii. JAMES W. BARKLEY, b. 1848; d. March 13, 1928, Clermont County, OH.
iii. THEODORE WILLIAM BARKLEY, b. September 04, 1853, New Richmond, Clermont County, Ohio; d. March 22, 1926, Baldwin City, Douglas, Kansas; m. ROSELLA AMANDA MOUNTS, September 06, 1891, White City, Morris County, Kansas; b. November 17, 1871, Wilsey, Morris, Kansas; d. August 15, 1956, Baldwin City, Douglas, Kansas.
iv. ASA TELL BARKLEY, b. March 1856, Clermont County, OH; m. ELIZABETH FRITZ.
v. HOSEA STILLMAN BARKLEY, b. June 30, 1859, New Richmond, Ohio; d. 1946; m. JULIA ENOS MOUNTS, December 11, 1892, Ash Grove, Greene County, Missouri.
vi. IDA BARKLEY, b. 1861.
vii. CHARLES C. BARKLEY, b. 1866, Clermont County, OH; d. 1941.

32. HENRY CARTER[6] BARKLEY *(JAMES M.[5], WILLIAM[4], GEORGE[3], JOHN[2] BARCLAY, DAVID BARCLAY OF[1] URIE)* was born December 02, 1827 in Clermont County, OH, and died November 12, 1892 in Clermont County, OH. He married (1) MELISSA BUSHMAN. She was born 1840, and died 1927. He married (2) BARBARA JANE CLARKE March 24, 1850 in Clermont County, Ohio, daughter of JOHN CLARKE. She was born 1832.

Notes for BARBARA JANE CLARKE:
Will to-wit:
Know all men by these presents that I Barbary Jane Barkley, of Clermont County, Ohio being of sound mind and memory and being desirous of settling my Godly affairs while I have strength and capacity to do so, do make and publish this my last Will and Testament; that is to say I give devise and bequeath to my beloved husband H. C. Barkley all the property both real and personal which I may die seized or possessed of every kind and description and I hereby especially devise give and bequeath to my said husband H. C. Barkley all my interests both real and personal in the estate of my father John Clark deceased. The same at deceased to me by said John Clark said real estate I give to my said husband in fee and authorizing him to sell and convey the same as he may hereafter wish. In witness whereof I have hereunto set my hand and seal this 27th day of September A.D. 1867. Barbary Jane (X) Barkley {Seal}
Signed and sealed by the said Barbary Jane Barkley as and for her last Will and Testament in the presence of us who in the presence of each other and at her request have hereunto set our names as witnesses. James K. Parker and Perry H. Barkley

Children of HENRY BARKLEY and MELISSA BUSHMAN are:

i. CLARENCE[7] BARKLEY, b. July 30, 1876.
ii. GEORGE CURTIS BARKLEY, b. July 17, 1871.

Children of HENRY BARKLEY and BARBARA CLARKE are:

iii. JOHN SPENCER[7] BARKLEY, b. October 04, 1852.
iv. MARY IDA BARKLEY, b. August 24, 1860.
v. ELLA CARTER BARKLEY, b. March 19, 1867.
vi. GEORGE CURTIS BARKLEY, b. July 27, 1871.
vii. MARIA BELLE BARKLEY, b. August 26, 1857.
viii. SARAH JANE BARKLEY, b. December 16, 1863.

33. JAMES M.[6] BARKLEY *(JAMES M.[5], WILLIAM[4], GEORGE[3], JOHN[2] BARCLAY, DAVID BARCLAY OF[1] URIE)* was born January 24, 1831 in Clermont County, OH, and died September 04, 1851 in Clermont County, OH. He married (1) ELIZABETH RICHARDS September 04, 1851 in Clermont County, Ohio. She was born 1833. He married (2) ELIZABETH/EVELYN RICHARDS September 04, 1851 in Clermont County, Ohio. She was born 1827 in Ohio, and died 1861.

Children of JAMES BARKLEY and ELIZABETH RICHARDS are:
37.   i.   JOSEPH HENRY LOUIS[7] BARKLEY, b. June 20, 1852, Clermont County, Ohio; d. June 22, 1931, Austin Twp., Cass County, Missouri.
     ii.   OLIVER G. BARKLEY, b. 1854.
     iii.   WILHELMINA JANE "MINA" BARKLEY, b. 1857; d. February 12, 1935, Lebanon, Laclede County, Missouri.
     iv.   SARAH B. BARKLEY, b. 1860.
     v.   JAMES BARKLEY, b. 1862.

34. MARY JANE[6] BARKLEY *(JOSEPH[5], WILLIAM[4], GEORGE[3], JOHN[2] BARCLAY, DAVID BARCLAY OF[1] URIE)* was born 1835 in Clermont County, OH. She married ANDREW HENRY HANNA February 21, 1860 in Clermont County, Ohio. He was born 1813.

Notes for MARY JANE BARKLEY:
She was born in 1835 so apparently stepmother to Hanna children.

Children of MARY BARKLEY and ANDREW HANNA are:
     i.   ELLISON[7] HANNA, b. 1845.
     ii.   THOMAS HANNA, b. 1850.
     iii.   CHARLES HANNA, b. 1853.
     iv.   ALICE HANNA, b. 1857.
     v.   MARY J. HANNA, b. 1860.

35. LUCY MAXWELL[6] BARKLEY *(JOSEPH[5], WILLIAM[4], GEORGE[3], JOHN[2] BARCLAY, DAVID BARCLAY OF[1] URIE)* was born September 15, 1841 in Washington Township, Clermont, Ohio, and died July 08, 1908 in Clermont County, OH. She married PETER CARMERER SMITH April 05, 1877 in Clermont County, Ohio, son of ISAREAL SMITH and BARBARA CARMERER. He was born 1837 in Big Indian Creek, Washington Township, Clermont County, Ohio, and died 1915 in Clermont County, OH.

Children of LUCY BARKLEY and PETER SMITH are:
     i.   SADIE[7] SMITH, b. February 07, 1878; m. WILLIAM A. WEDDING.
     ii.   LAURA A. SMITH, b. April 03, 1880; m. G. E. DENNISTON, November 28, 1912.
     iii.   JESSIE L. SMITH, b. October 1884; m. EUGENE DENNISTON, November 28, 1912.

Generation No. 7

36. WILLIAM HENRY[7] BARKLEY *(GEORGE WASHINGTON[6], ANDREW[5], JOSEPH[4], GEORGE[3], JOHN[2] BARCLAY, DAVID BARCLAY OF[1] URIE)* was born 1858 in Ohio, and died 1927 in Texas. He married MABEL V. ELLIS. She was born March 14, 1847 in Texas, and died January 12, 1966 in Texas.

Child of WILLIAM BARKLEY and MABEL ELLIS is:
38.   i.   WILLARD[8] HENRY, JR. BARKLEY, b. September 29, 1908, Texas; d. February 07, 1976, Texas.

37. JOSEPH HENRY LOUIS[7] BARKLEY *(JAMES M.[6], JAMES M.[5], WILLIAM[4], GEORGE[3], JOHN[2] BARCLAY, DAVID BARCLAY OF[1] URIE)* was born June 20, 1852 in Clermont County, Ohio, and died June 22, 1931 in Austin Twp., Cass County, Missouri. He married MARY ELIZABETH BARBER, daughter of HARVEY BARBER and LOUISA MANNING. She was born April 01, 1862 in Ohio, and died July 01, 1930 in Archie, Cass County, MO.

Notes for JOSEPH HENRY LOUIS BARKLEY:
Marriage record Bates County, Butler, Missouri: Book 1871-1881, Book 3, Page 221.
"State of Missouri, County of Bates, June 14th A.D. 1881. This is to certify that on the 14th day of June A.D. 1881 Mr. Joseph H. Barkley and Miss Mary E. Barber were by me UNITED IN MARRIAGE, according to the laws of God and of the State of Missouri, at the residence of H. J. Barber, Bates County, Missouri. Thomas . Holand, Justice of the Peace. Filed for Record in this office on the 29th of June, 1881. Jas. L. Pace, Recorder, by A. B. Simms, Deputy."

More About JOSEPH HENRY LOUIS BARKLEY:
Burial: Mt. Olivet Cemetery, SE of Adrian, Missouri

More About MARY ELIZABETH BARBER:
Burial: Mt. Olivet Cemetery SE of Adrian, Missouri, Bates County

Children of JOSEPH BARKLEY and MARY BARBER are:

      i.   RENA B.⁸ BARKLEY, b. September 1882; d. 1935.

         Notes for RENA B. BARKLEY:
         Rena was a gifted child and never married.

         More About RENA B. BARKLEY:
         Burial: Lebanon, Missouri

39.   ii.   STELLA MAE BARKLEY, b. August 03, 1884, Archie, Cass County, MO; d. June 22, 1971, Lebanon, Laclede County, Missouri.

     iii.   OREN PERRY BARKLEY, b. August 20, 1886, Archie, Missouri; d. April 24, 1959, Archie, Missouri.

         Notes for OREN PERRY BARKLEY:
         Services April 29, 1959, Archie Baptist Church, Rev. Kenneth Edmonson, Atkinson-Dicky Funera Home, Archie, Missouri. Oren never married; he became a hobo and traveled on the railroad trains. He would stop in Adrian or Butler, Missouri, and contact his sister, Nellie, so they could visit.

         More About OREN PERRY BARKLEY:
         Burial: Mt. Olivet Cemetery, SE of Adrian, Missouri

     iv.   JOSEPHINE EDNA BARKLEY, b. June 08, 1888, Everett Twp., Cass County, Missouri; d. 1932; m. JOE MINARICK.

         Notes for JOSEPHINE EDNA BARKLEY:
         Poisoned with arsenic; murder never solved, brother-in-law Arthur Kirkner suspected over property dispute. Her body was cremated.

40.   v.   ARTHUR HARRISON BARKLEY, b. November 10, 1889; d. January 16, 1974, Wichita, Kansas.

41.   vi.   ELIZABETH JAY BARKLEY, b. October 19, 1893, Everett Twp., Cass County, Missouri; d. May 1975, St. Joseph, Missouri.

     vii.   ALMA MYRTLE BARKLEY, b. June 09, 1895, Everett Twp., Cass County, Missouri; d. February 16, 1988, Kansas City, Missouri; m. ARTHUR KIRKNER; b. April 16, 1881; d. June 04, 1921, Kansas City, Missouri.

         Notes for ALMA MYRTLE BARKLEY:
         No children. First lived in Stockton, Missouri; then moved to Kansas City, Missouri. Arthur was cremated February 16, 1959; Alma kept his ashes under her bed in an urn.

         More About ALMA MYRTLE BARKLEY:
         Burial: February 19, 1988, Mt. Moriah Cemetery, Kansas City, Missouri

    viii.   MARION HARVEY BARKLEY, b. June 05, 1898, Missouri; d. Independence, Missouri; m. RUBY MOBERLY.

         Notes for MARION HARVEY BARKLEY:
         He was in World War I Signal Corps. No children.

         More About MARION HARVEY BARKLEY:
         Burial: Woodlawn Cemetery, Independence, Missouri

     ix.   NELLIE BARKLEY¹, b. August 06, 1900, Union City, Cass County, Missouri; d. October 27, 1948; m. UFA HENRY DURBIN¹, June 30, 1923, Bates County, Missouri; b. November 08, 1899, Effingham County, Moccasin Twp., IL; d. March 04, 1958, Butler, Missouri, Bates County, MO.

         Notes for NELLIE BARKLEY:
         Married in home of Ufa's parents, Lewis Durbin and Laura Ewing.

More About NELLIE BARKLEY:
Burial: Oak Hill Cemetery, Butler, Missouri

Notes for UFA HENRY DURBIN:
See Book 3: Descendants of Samuel and Elizabeth Heathcote for children of Ufa Henry Durbin and Nellie Barkley.

More About UFA HENRY DURBIN:
Burial: Oak Hill Cemetery, Butler, Missouri

    x.   BERNIECE NAOMI BARKLEY, b. December 28, 1902, Everett, Cass County, Missouri; d. May 07, 1989, Kansas City, Missouri; m. BRUCE ADAMS.

Notes for BERNIECE NAOMI BARKLEY:
He divorced her for another woman; she never remarried. Lived at 2533 Askew, Kansas City, Missouri; house where she and husband, Bruce Adams, had lived. Sister Alma Myrtle lived with her after death of husband, Arthur Kirkner.

More About BERNIECE NAOMI BARKLEY:
Burial: May 11, 1989, Mt. Moriah Cemetery, Kansas City, Missouri

42.   xi.   NELLIE BARKLEY, b. August 11, 1900, Union City, MO; d. October 27, 1948, Bates County, MO.

Generation No. 8

38. WILLARD[8] HENRY, JR. BARKLEY *(WILLIAM HENRY[7] BARKLEY, GEORGE WASHINGTON[6], ANDREW[5], JOSEPH[4], GEORGE[3], JOHN[2] BARCLAY, DAVID BARCLAY OF[1] URIE)* was born September 29, 1908 in Texas, and died February 07, 1976 in Texas. He married REVARLLE BEALER. She was born August 30, 1910 in Texas, and died July 23, 1981 in Texas.

Child of WILLARD HENRY and REVARLLE BEALER is:
43.   i.   FRED WILLIAM[9] BARKLEY, b. August 11, 1940, Texas; d. January 01, 1996, Texas.

39. STELLA MAE[8] BARKLEY *(JOSEPH HENRY LOUIS[7], JAMES M.[6], JAMES M.[5], WILLIAM[4], GEORGE[3], JOHN[2] BARCLAY, DAVID BARCLAY OF[1] URIE)* was born August 03, 1884 in Archie, Cass County, MO, and died June 22, 1971 in Lebanon, Laclede County, Missouri. She married (1) ORRIS ESTES in Stockton, Missouri. She married (2) CAL CHASTAIN.

Notes for STELLA MAE BARKLEY:
No children; Calvin Chastain was stepson.

Notes for CAL CHASTAIN:
They lived near Lebanon, Missouri. Calvin, Jr. killed in automobile accident. Father learned of his death on TV.

Child of STELLA BARKLEY and CAL CHASTAIN is:
    i.   CALVIN[9] CHASTAIN, JR..

       Notes for CALVIN CHASTAIN, JR.:
       Killed in automobile accident. Father learned of death while watching TV.

40. ARTHUR HARRISON[8] BARKLEY *(JOSEPH HENRY LOUIS[7], JAMES M.[6], JAMES M.[5], WILLIAM[4], GEORGE[3], JOHN[2] BARCLAY, DAVID BARCLAY OF[1] URIE)* was born November 10, 1889, and died January 16, 1974 in Wichita, Kansas. He married MARY ALETHA STEELE. She was born in Boscobel, Wisconsin.

Children of ARTHUR BARKLEY and MARY STEELE are:
44.   i.   HARRY ARTHUR[9] BARKLEY.

45.   ii.   ROBERT LOUIS BARKLEY.

41. ELIZABETH JAY[8] BARKLEY (*JOSEPH HENRY LOUIS*[7], *JAMES M.*[6], *JAMES M.*[5], *WILLIAM*[4], *GEORGE*[3], *JOHN*[2] *BARCLAY, DAVID BARCLAY OF*[1] *URIE*) was born October 19, 1893 in Everett Twp., Cass County, Missouri, and died May 1975 in St. Joseph, Missouri. She married HARRY BEAUFORT.

More About ELIZABETH JAY BARKLEY:
Burial: St. Mary's Cemetery, St. Joseph, Missouri

Children of ELIZABETH BARKLEY and HARRY BEAUFORT are:
          i.   HARRY[9] BEAUFORT, JR..

               Notes for HARRY BEAUFORT, JR.:
               He had three girls and 3 boys; 1 daughter murdered--no details.

46.   ii.   DOROTHY BEAUFORT, b. October 08, 1920, St. Joseph, Missouri.
47.   iii.   ROBERT LEWIS BEAUFORT.

42. NELLIE[8] BARKLEY (*JOSEPH HENRY LOUIS*[7], *JAMES M.*[6], *JAMES M.*[5], *WILLIAM*[4], *GEORGE*[3], *JOHN*[2] *BARCLAY, DAVID BARCLAY OF*[1] *URIE*) was born August 11, 1900 in Union City, MO, and died October 27, 1948 in Bates County, MO. She married UFA HENRY DURBIN[1] June 30, 1923 in Home of his parents, son of LOUIS DURBIN and LAURA EWING. He was born November 08, 1899 in Effingham County, Moccasin Twp., IL, and died March 04, 1958 in Butler, Missouri, Bates County, MO.

More About NELLIE BARKLEY:
Burial: Oak Hill Cemetery, Butler, Missouri

Notes for UFA HENRY DURBIN:
See Book 3: Descendants of Samuel and Elizabeth Heathcote for children of Ufa Henry Durbin and Nellie Barkley.

More About UFA HENRY DURBIN:
Burial: Oak Hill Cemetery, Butler, Missouri

Children of NELLIE BARKLEY and UFA DURBIN are:
48.   i.   MARVIN DARRELL[9] DURBIN, b. April 08, 1924, Butler, Missouri, Bates County, MO; d. December 11, 1992, Seattle, King County, Washington.
49.   ii.   JACK CALVIN DURBIN, b. September 23, 1925, Bates County, Missouri; d. January 18, 2012, Wichita, Sedgewick, Kansas.
         iii.   LEONARD LEROY DURBIN, b. August 20, 1927, Bates County, Missouri; d. February 05, 1995, Butler, Missouri, Bates County, MO.

               Notes for LEONARD LEROY DURBIN:
               Never married. Buried beside parents. He was a mechanic and owned many old cars.

               His name is listed as Leonard Leroy Barkley on the census record; mother and father temporarily separated.

               More About LEONARD LEROY DURBIN:
               Burial: Oak Hill Cemetery, Butler, Missouri

50.   iv.   BETTY JEWELL DURBIN, b. February 02, 1931, Bates County, MO.
51.   v.   DORIS MAY DURBIN, b. August 11, 1932, Butler, Missouri, Bates County, MO; d. February 04, 2014, Alvin, Texas.
52.   vi.   PEGGY JOYCE DURBIN, b. July 02, 1936.
53.   vii.   CAROL JEAN DURBIN, b. July 01, 1940.

Generation No. 9

43. FRED WILLIAM[9] BARKLEY *(WILLARD[8] HENRY, JR. BARKLEY, WILLIAM HENRY[7] BARKLEY, GEORGE WASHINGTON[6], ANDREW[5], JOSEPH[4], GEORGE[3], JOHN[2] BARCLAY, DAVID BARCLAY OF[1] URIE)* was born August 11, 1940 in Texas, and died January 01, 1996 in Texas.

Child of FRED WILLIAM BARKLEY is:
  i.   RANDY A.[10] BARKLEY, b. December 21, 1964, Angelina County, Texas; d. June 09, 2002, Lufkin, Texas; m. PRIVATE, May 31, 1986, Angelina County, Texas.

44. HARRY ARTHUR[9] BARKLEY *(ARTHUR HARRISON[8], JOSEPH HENRY LOUIS[7], JAMES M.[6], JAMES M.[5], WILLIAM[4], GEORGE[3], JOHN[2] BARCLAY, DAVID BARCLAY OF[1] URIE)* He married MARGARET DOUGLAS. She was born in Douglas, Kansas.

Child of HARRY BARKLEY and MARGARET DOUGLAS is:
  i.   STEVE[10] BARKLEY.

       Notes for STEVE BARKLEY:
       Lived in Belton, Missouri in 1990. Inherited his Aunt Bernice's property.

45. ROBERT LOUIS[9] BARKLEY *(ARTHUR HARRISON[8], JOSEPH HENRY LOUIS[7], JAMES M.[6], JAMES M.[5], WILLIAM[4], GEORGE[3], JOHN[2] BARCLAY, DAVID BARCLAY OF[1] URIE)* He married ANNA MAY.

Notes for ROBERT LOUIS BARKLEY:
Lived in Haysville, Kansas in 1990

Children of ROBERT BARKLEY and ANNA MAY are:
  i.   KENNY[10] BARKLEY.
  ii. BRADLEY BARKLEY.

46. DOROTHY[9] BEAUFORT *(ELIZABETH JAY[8] BARKLEY, JOSEPH HENRY LOUIS[7], JAMES M.[6], JAMES M.[5], WILLIAM[4], GEORGE[3], JOHN[2] BARCLAY, DAVID BARCLAY OF[1] URIE)* was born October 08, 1920 in St. Joseph, Missouri. She married (1) SPIVEY. She married (2) KELLY.

Notes for DOROTHY BEAUFORT:
Husband killed in World War II. No children. Lived in Atlanta, GA in 1977.

Children of DOROTHY BEAUFORT and SPIVEY are:
  i.   KEITH DOUGLAS[10] SPIVEY, b. July 26, 1948.
  ii. GLYNN LYNEAU SPIVEY, b. March 03, 1951.

47. ROBERT LEWIS[9] BEAUFORT *(ELIZABETH JAY[8] BARKLEY, JOSEPH HENRY LOUIS[7], JAMES M.[6], JAMES M.[5], WILLIAM[4], GEORGE[3], JOHN[2] BARCLAY, DAVID BARCLAY OF[1] URIE)* He married FAIRY. She died 1977.

Children of ROBERT BEAUFORT and FAIRY are:
  i.   GALEN[10] BEAUFORT.
  ii. BECKY BEAUFORT.

48. MARVIN DARRELL[9] DURBIN *(NELLIE[8] BARKLEY, JOSEPH HENRY LOUIS[7], JAMES M.[6], JAMES M.[5], WILLIAM[4], GEORGE[3], JOHN[2] BARCLAY, DAVID BARCLAY OF[1] URIE)* was born April 08, 1924 in Butler, Missouri, Bates County, MO, and died December 11, 1992 in Seattle, King County, Washington. He married (1) SUSAN MAE WEBSTER. She was born November 22, 1946 in Sand Point, Idaho. He married (2) JOAN LaDUKE. He married (3) BETTY LEE SCHMIDT August 04, 1948, daughter of JOHN SCHMIDT and LENA GREEN.

Notes for MARVIN DARRELL DURBIN:
Cremated.

More About MARVIN DARRELL DURBIN:
Burial: Forest Lawn Cemetery, Seattle, Washington

Notes for SUSAN MAE WEBSTER:
Marvin and Susan divorced in 1979; she remarried; died of breast cancer, funeral held in Couer d'Alene, Idaho.

Children of MARVIN DURBIN and SUSAN WEBSTER are:
    i.   VICTORIA LYNN[10] DURBIN, b. February 26, 1966.
    ii.   TAMARA SUE DURBIN, b. February 13, 1974.

        Notes for TAMARA SUE DURBIN:
        She was an adopted child.

Children of MARVIN DURBIN and JOAN LADUKE are:
    iii.   DONNA RAE[10] LADUKE, b. March 26, 1957.
    iv.   RICHARD LEE LADUKE, b. August 12, 1960.

Children of MARVIN DURBIN and BETTY SCHMIDT are:
    v.   DARRELL LEE[10] DURBIN, b. July 14, 1948.
    vi.   CAROLYN SUE DURBIN, b. July 08, 1949, Kansas City, Missouri; d. July 04, 1957, Milan, Kansas.

        Notes for CAROLYN SUE DURBIN:
        Killed by roof falling from porch; poor construction.

        More About CAROLYN SUE DURBIN:
        Burial: Oak Hill Cemetery, Butler, Missouri

    vii.   DAVID LAWRENCE DURBIN, d. April 03, 1996.

        Notes for DAVID LAWRENCE DURBIN:
        Adopted, b. at St. Luke's Hospital, Sumner, Kansas, delivered by Dr. P. G. Price. His birth father's name was
        Craig, mother Marilyn Hagon, alias Mrs. Lee Youngblood, Ft. Scott, Pine St., Kansas. David had a sister by
        same parents; adopted name Patricia Ann Hagon. Couple at Ft. Scott, KS adopted her and moved to
        California. David lived with his adopted mother, Betty Lee, in Victoria, Texas.
        Graduate of Calhoun High School and Vogue College of Cosometology.
        Died April 3, 1996. Survivors: mother and stepfather, Betty L. Schmidt Durbin, Pass Reid and James A.
        Reid of Port Lavaca; brothers Albert L. Pass of Seattle, WA; Jessie Clint Pass of Strowsburg, PA; Bill Pass III
        of Denton, TX; MSGT Darrell L. Durbin, Wiley, Texas.

        More About DAVID LAWRENCE DURBIN:
        Burial: Oak Hill Cemetery, Butler, Missouri

49. JACK CALVIN[9] DURBIN (*NELLIE[8] BARKLEY, JOSEPH HENRY LOUIS[7], JAMES M.[6], JAMES M.[5], WILLIAM[4], GEORGE[3], JOHN[2] BARCLAY, DAVID BARCLAY OF[1] URIE*) was born September 23, 1925 in Bates County, Missouri, and died January 18, 2012 in Wichita, Sedgewick, Kansas. He married MAE DEAN WOOLEY, daughter of OVID WOOLEY and MILDRED WALKER. She was born September 07, 1928 in Mangum, Greer County, Oklahoma, and died August 23, 2010 in Wichita, Sedgewick, Kansas.

More About JACK CALVIN DURBIN:
Burial: Wichita Park Cemetery

More About MAE DEAN WOOLEY:
Burial: Wichita Park Cemetery

Children of JACK DURBIN and MAE WOOLEY are:
    i.   DOROTHY ANNETTE[10] DURBIN, b. September 1955, Wichita, Sedgewick, Kansas; d. September 1955, Wichita, Sedgewick, Kansas.

        Notes for DOROTHY ANNETTE DURBIN:
        Twin to Debra Jeanette, died at birth.

        More About DOROTHY ANNETTE DURBIN:
        Burial: Wichita Park Cemetery

    ii.   DEBRA JEANETTE DURBIN, b. September 1955.
    iii. BLAKE CALVIN DURBIN, b. February 11, 1967.

        Notes for BLAKE CALVIN DURBIN:
        Adopted from mixed blood parents.

50. BETTY JEWELL[9] DURBIN *(NELLIE[8] BARKLEY, JOSEPH HENRY LOUIS[7], JAMES M.[6], JAMES M.[5], WILLIAM[4], GEORGE[3], JOHN[2] BARCLAY, DAVID BARCLAY OF[1] URIE)* was born February 02, 1931 in Bates County, MO. She married WINFRED LEE CARSON, SR. July 14, 1949 in Independence, MO, son of REUBEN CARSON and CORA SAUNDERS. He was born August 15, 1920 in Cherryvale, KS, and died August 09, 1991 in VA Hospital, Columbia, MO.

More About WINFRED LEE CARSON, SR.:
Burial: Cremated, ashes scattered Sassafras Mt., SC

Children of BETTY DURBIN and WINFRED CARSON are:
54.   i.   WINFRED LEE[10] CARSON, JR., b. May 08, 1954, Butler, Missouri, Bates County, MO.
55.   ii.   BONNIE LEE CARSON, b. September 28, 1957, Butler, Missouri, Bates County, MO.

51. DORIS MAY[9] DURBIN *(NELLIE[8] BARKLEY, JOSEPH HENRY LOUIS[7], JAMES M.[6], JAMES M.[5], WILLIAM[4], GEORGE[3], JOHN[2] BARCLAY, DAVID BARCLAY OF[1] URIE)* was born August 11, 1932 in Butler, Missouri, Bates County, MO, and died February 04, 2014 in Alvin, Texas. She married OVID MAURICE WOOLEY February 17, 1952 in Wichita, Kansas, son of OVID WOOLEY and MILDRED WALKER. He was born July 03, 1933 in Happy, Texas, and died November 05, 2004 in Rosharon, Brazoria, Texas.

Notes for DORIS MAY DURBIN:
Married in home of brother, Jack Calvin Durbin and Mae Dean Wooley Durbin; Ovid and Mae Dean were brother and sister.

Ashes scattered over parents' graves, Oak Hill Cemetery, Butler, Missouri.

Notes for OVID MAURICE WOOLEY:
Ashes scattered in field, Happy, Texas

More About OVID MAURICE WOOLEY:
Burial: Happy, Texas

Children of DORIS DURBIN and OVID WOOLEY are:
56.   i.   MARTHA ANN[10] WOOLEY, b. January 02, 1953, Wichita, Sedgewick, Kansas.
           ii.   OVID MAURICE WOOLEY, JR., b. November 15, 1955.
57.   iii. RICHARD LYNN WOOLEY, b. February 21, 1959, Mangum, Greer County, Oklahoma.
           iv.   BEVERLY SUE WOOLEY, b. April 26, 1962.
58.   v.   PEGGY JEAN WOOLEY, b. November 26, 1964, Mangum, Greer County, Oklahoma.

52. PEGGY JOYCE[9] DURBIN *(NELLIE[8] BARKLEY, JOSEPH HENRY LOUIS[7], JAMES M.[6], JAMES M.[5], WILLIAM[4],*

GEORGE[3], *JOHN*[2] *BARCLAY, DAVID BARCLAY OF*[1] *URIE)*[1] was born July 02, 1936. She married IRVIN LEE BEERY[1] July 02, 1955 in Wichita, Kansas, USA; Marriage: St. Paul's Lutheran Church[1], son of IVEN BEERY and VERNOLA LAIRD. He was born February 26, 1934 in Ringling, Jefferson, Oklahoma, USA[1], and died October 25, 2012 in Wichita, Sedgwick, Kansas, USA[1].

Children of PEGGY DURBIN and IRVIN BEERY are:

59. i. VICKI LYNN[10] BEERY, b. December 17, 1956, Wichita, Sedgwick, Kansas, USA; St. Joseph Hospital.
60. ii. CYNTHIA DIANE BEERY, b. December 28, 1958, Wichita, Sedgwick, Kansas, USA; St. Joseph Hospital.
61. iii. CHERYL DENISE BEERY, b. March 26, 1963, Wichita, Sedgwick, Kansas, USA; St. Joseph Hospital.

53. CAROL JEAN[9] DURBIN *(NELLIE*[8] *BARKLEY, JOSEPH HENRY LOUIS*[7], *JAMES M.*[6], *JAMES M.*[5], *WILLIAM*[4], *GEORGE*[3], *JOHN*[2] *BARCLAY, DAVID BARCLAY OF*[1] *URIE)* was born July 01, 1940. She married ARTHUR BIDNER March 03, 1962 in Kansas City, Missouri, son of SIDNEY BIDNER and ROSE LEVY. He was born February 17, 1932 in Brooklyn, New York.

Child of CAROL DURBIN and ARTHUR BIDNER is:

62. i. SUSAN JEANETTE[10] BIDNER, b. August 28, 1963.

Generation No. 10

54. WINFRED LEE[10] CARSON, JR. *(BETTY JEWELL*[9] *DURBIN, NELLIE*[8] *BARKLEY, JOSEPH HENRY LOUIS*[7], *JAMES M.*[6], *JAMES M.*[5], *WILLIAM*[4], *GEORGE*[3], *JOHN*[2] *BARCLAY, DAVID BARCLAY OF*[1] *URIE)* was born May 08, 1954 in Butler, Missouri, Bates County, MO. He married SANDA KANDI February 1979 in Central Baptist Church, Fayetteville, Arkansas. She was born October 21, 1946 in South Pelak, Teluk Anson 34 Canal Road, Malaysia.

Notes for SANDA KANDI:
Parents migrated from India before she was born. Her Indian name is Chandra Davi, d/o Singgaram Pather, s/o Kolinda Villos and Kamelah, d/o Sanggaram; first daughter.
She attended the Convent of the Holy Infant Jesus National Type Secondary School (English) at Teluk Anson from /9/1953 to 4/12/1964. Sat for Cambridge School Exam in 1964. On September 2, 1970, granted admission to the Stamford & Rutland Hospital as a student nurse; graduated with high honors March 24, 1975. Received title of "Registered Nurse" by the General Nursing Council for England and Wales. Came to United States in1977 with other nurses with whom she had graduated to work in a nursing home in Fayetteville, Arkansas where she met her future husband.
She began working as a RN at Palmetto Baptist Medical Center, Columbia, SC in the maternity ward taking care of new mothers in 1981; she retired in 2016.

Children of WINFRED CARSON and SANDA KANDI are:

63. i. TERRANCE DALE[11] CARSON, b. February 06, 1979, Portland, Oregon.
     ii. JASON LEE CARSON, b. June 25, 1981, Umatilla, Oregon.

     Notes for JASON LEE CARSON:
     First child to be born in new birthing chair at hospital where his mother was a Registered Nurse.

     iii. NICOLE NEELA CARSON, b. June 30, 1988, Kansas City, Missouri.

     Notes for NICOLE NEELA CARSON:
     Graduate of University of Charleston, South Carolina.

55. BONNIE LEE[10] CARSON *(BETTY JEWELL*[9] *DURBIN, NELLIE*[8] *BARKLEY, JOSEPH HENRY LOUIS*[7], *JAMES M.*[6], *JAMES M.*[5], *WILLIAM*[4], *GEORGE*[3], *JOHN*[2] *BARCLAY, DAVID BARCLAY OF*[1] *URIE)* was born September 28, 1957 in Butler, Missouri, Bates County, MO. She married (1) ROBERT WILLIAM JOHNSON December 20, 1977 in Central Baptist Church, Fayetteville, Arkansas. She married (2) KEVIN LEE PECK August 02, 1982 in Tulsa, Oklahoma. She married (3) DANIEL MILLER July 1990 in Tulsa, Oklahoma.

Child of BONNIE CARSON and DANIEL MILLER is:
      i.   DANIEL LEE[11] MILLER, b. April 14, 2000.

56. MARTHA ANN[10] WOOLEY *(DORIS MAY[9] DURBIN, NELLIE[8] BARKLEY, JOSEPH HENRY LOUIS[7], JAMES M.[6], JAMES M.[5], WILLIAM[4], GEORGE[3], JOHN[2] BARCLAY, DAVID BARCLAY OF[1] URIE)* was born January 02, 1953 in Wichita, Sedgewick, Kansas. She married PAUL JOHN BARTHELOME VOLCHERICK January 09, 1973.

Child of MARTHA WOOLEY and PAUL VOLCHERICK is:
      i.   LANE EDWARD[11] VOLCHERICK, b. June 08, 1980.

57. RICHARD LYNN[10] WOOLEY *(DORIS MAY[9] DURBIN, NELLIE[8] BARKLEY, JOSEPH HENRY LOUIS[7], JAMES M.[6], JAMES M.[5], WILLIAM[4], GEORGE[3], JOHN[2] BARCLAY, DAVID BARCLAY OF[1] URIE)* was born February 21, 1959 in Mangum, Greer County, Oklahoma. He married (1) BRENDA KAY MILLER. She was born January 27, 1961. He married (2) RHONDA ROBBERSON September 18, 1981.

Children of RICHARD WOOLEY and BRENDA MILLER are:
      i.   JASON NEIL[11] WOOLEY, b. April 26, 1976.

             Notes for JASON NEIL WOOLEY:
             Adopted in 1989.

     ii.   KAVEH MARLIN WOOLEY, b. January 09, 1978.

             Notes for KAVEH MARLIN WOOLEY:
             Adopted in1989. Brother to Jason Neil Wooley.

    iii.   KAPRIL MICHELLE WOOLEY, b. October 07, 1987, Wurtsmith AFB, Iosco County, Michigan.

Child of RICHARD WOOLEY and RHONDA ROBBERSON is:
    iv.   LARRY[11] ROBBERSON, b. August 02, 1977, Grand Prairie, Texas.

             Notes for LARRY ROBBERSON:
             Stepchild of Richard Lynn Wooley.

58. PEGGY JEAN[10] WOOLEY *(DORIS MAY[9] DURBIN, NELLIE[8] BARKLEY, JOSEPH HENRY LOUIS[7], JAMES M.[6], JAMES M.[5], WILLIAM[4], GEORGE[3], JOHN[2] BARCLAY, DAVID BARCLAY OF[1] URIE)* was born November 26, 1964 in Mangum, Greer County, Oklahoma. She married RICKY DEAN SHAWBACK October 01, 1983, son of RAY SHAWBACK and PHILLIS LAUNE.

Children of PEGGY WOOLEY and RICKY SHAWBACK are:
      i.   PEGGY LEEANN[11] SHAWBACK, b. April 09, 1984.
     ii.   CHRYSTAL MAY SHAWBACK, b. January 13, 1986.
    iii.   LAUANE MARRIE SHAWBACK, b. January 19, 1988.

59. VICKI LYNN[10] BEERY *(PEGGY JOYCE[9] DURBIN, NELLIE[8] BARKLEY, JOSEPH HENRY LOUIS[7], JAMES M.[6], JAMES M.[5], WILLIAM[4], GEORGE[3], JOHN[2] BARCLAY, DAVID BARCLAY OF[1] URIE)[1]* was born December 17, 1956 in Wichita, Sedgwick, Kansas, USA; St. Joseph Hospital[1]. She married JERRY ALLAN SMITH[1] May 17, 1980 in Wichita, Sedgwick, Kansas, USA; Marriage: Olivet Baptist Church[1], son of LARNARD SMITH and EVA MILLER. He was born February 17, 1954[1].

Children of VICKI BEERY and JERRY SMITH are:
      i.   ANDREW PHILIP[11] SMITH[1], b. December 21, 1985, Liberal, Seward, Kansas, USA[1].
64.   ii.   ANNA ELIZABETH SMITH, b. September 24, 1987, Liberal, Seward, Kansas, USA.
    iii.   LYDIA ABIGAIL SMITH[1], b. February 22, 1991, Liberal, Seward, Kansas, USA[1]; m. AARON CRESS[1], June

05, 2010, Andover, Butler, Kansas, USA; Marriage: Faith Baptist Church[1]; b. February 20, 1991[1].
  iv. LEAH RACHEL SMITH[1], b. November 23, 1992, Liberal, Seward, Kansas, USA[1].

60. CYNTHIA DIANE[10] BEERY *(PEGGY JOYCE[9] DURBIN, NELLIE[8] BARKLEY, JOSEPH HENRY LOUIS[7], JAMES M.[6], JAMES M.[5], WILLIAM[4], GEORGE[3], JOHN[2] BARCLAY, DAVID BARCLAY OF[1] URIE)[1]* was born December 28, 1958 in Wichita, Sedgwick, Kansas, USA; St. Joseph Hospital[1]. She married KARL WARREN BAUDER[1] May 21, 1983 in Wichita, Sedgwick, Kansas, USA; Marriage: Olivet Baptist Church[1], son of DON BAUDER and PATRICIA BETHEL. He was born November 16, 1954 in Hutchiinson, KS[1].

Children of CYNTHIA BEERY and KARL BAUDER are:
65.   i. AARON THOMAS[11] BAUDER, b. August 02, 1988, Wichita, Sedgwick, Kansas, USA.
66.   ii. JOSHUA RYAN BAUDER, b. August 24, 1985, Wichita, Sedgwick, Kansas, USA; Wesley.

61. CHERYL DENISE[10] BEERY *(PEGGY JOYCE[9] DURBIN, NELLIE[8] BARKLEY, JOSEPH HENRY LOUIS[7], JAMES M.[6], JAMES M.[5], WILLIAM[4], GEORGE[3], JOHN[2] BARCLAY, DAVID BARCLAY OF[1] URIE)[1]* was born March 26, 1963 in Wichita, Sedgwick, Kansas, USA; St. Joseph Hospital[1]. She married (1) LARRY PHILIP SHELL JR.[1] August 18, 1984 in Wichita, Sedgwick, Kansas, USA; Marriage: Olivet Baptist Church[1], son of LARRY SHELL and EUNICE PATZEL. He was born August 20, 1962[1]. She married (2) DICK ALDES HOLIHAN JR.[1] March 16, 2016 in Frisco, Denton, Texas, USA[1], son of DICK HOLIHAN and FRANCES KELLY. He was born November 16, 1956 in Indianapolis, Hamilton, Indiana, USA; Ft. Benjamin Harrison[1].

Children of CHERYL BEERY and LARRY SHELL are:
      i. LAUREN ASHLEY[11] SHELL[1], b. December 04, 1987, Wichita, Sedgwick, Kansas, USA; Wesley Hospital[1].

        Notes for LAUREN ASHLEY SHELL:
        2016: Fiance' Cody Taylor, born 5/20/1988

67.   ii. JILLIAN LEIGH SHELL, b. December 18, 1989, Wichita, Sedgwick, Kansas, USA; Wesley Hospital.

62. SUSAN JEANETTE[10] BIDNER *(CAROL JEAN[9] DURBIN, NELLIE[8] BARKLEY, JOSEPH HENRY LOUIS[7], JAMES M.[6], JAMES M.[5], WILLIAM[4], GEORGE[3], JOHN[2] BARCLAY, DAVID BARCLAY OF[1] URIE)* was born August 28, 1963. She married JAMES EDWARD BURNS May 18, 1994 in Easton, Massachusetts. He was born January 22, 1964 in Farmington, Massachusetts.

Child of SUSAN BIDNER and JAMES BURNS is:
      i. BENJAMIN ALEXANDER[11] BURNS, b. February 13, 2002, Boston, Massachusetts.

Generation No. 11

63. TERRANCE DALE[11] CARSON *(WINFRED LEE[10], BETTY JEWELL[9] DURBIN, NELLIE[8] BARKLEY, JOSEPH HENRY LOUIS[7], JAMES M.[6], JAMES M.[5], WILLIAM[4], GEORGE[3], JOHN[2] BARCLAY, DAVID BARCLAY OF[1] URIE)* was born February 06, 1979 in Portland, Oregon. He married DIONNE PETERSEN February 2001 in Lexington, Lexington County, South Carolina, daughter of DONALD RHODES and DONNA RICHBURG.

Notes for TERRANCE DALE CARSON:
Born while mother was in Portland, Oregon, processing citizenship papers; she, husband, and baby traveled home by bus to Umatilla, Oregon, the next day.

He and Dionne divorced in 2006; he got primary custody of children.

Children of TERRANCE CARSON and DIONNE PETERSEN are:
      i. TYLER DALE[12] CARSON, b. September 14, 1999.
      ii. TAYLOR NICHOLE CARSON, b. February 13, 2002.
      iii. TIFFANIE JEAN CARSON, b. December 10, 2002.

64. ANNA ELIZABETH[11] SMITH *(VICKI LYNN[10] BEERY, PEGGY JOYCE[9] DURBIN, NELLIE[8] BARKLEY, JOSEPH HENRY LOUIS[7], JAMES M.[6], JAMES M.[5], WILLIAM[4], GEORGE[3], JOHN[2] BARCLAY, DAVID BARCLAY OF[1] URIE)[1]* was born September 24, 1987 in Liberal, Seward, Kansas, USA[1]. She married NOAH DANIEL MCLAUGHLIN[1] June 28, 2008 in Andover, Butler, Kansas, USA; Marriage: Faith Baptist Church[1], son of DAVID MCLAUGHLIN and JENNIFER MARTIN. He was born August 22, 1984[1].

Children of ANNA SMITH and NOAH MCLAUGHLIN are:
- i. HARLEY LYNE[12] MCLAUGHLIN[1], b. November 13, 2009, Wichita, Sedgwick, Kansas, USA; St. Joseph Hospital[1].
- ii. TRISTIN ROBERT LEE MCLAUGHLIN[1], b. July 09, 2011, Wichita, Sedgwick, Kansas, USA; St. Joseph Hospital[1]; d. December 21, 2011, El Dorado, Butler, Kansas, USA; Twin to Rustin, Died of SIDS[1].
- iii. RUSTIN RAE MCLAUGHLIN[1], b. July 09, 2011, Wichita, Sedgwick, Kansas, USA; St. Joseph Hospital, twin to Tristin[1].
- iv. HOPE ELIZABETH MCLAUGHLIN[1], b. December 03, 2012, Wichita, Sedgwick, Kansas, USA; St. Joseph Hospital[1].

65. AARON THOMAS[11] BAUDER *(CYNTHIA DIANE[10] BEERY, PEGGY JOYCE[9] DURBIN, NELLIE[8] BARKLEY, JOSEPH HENRY LOUIS[7], JAMES M.[6], JAMES M.[5], WILLIAM[4], GEORGE[3], JOHN[2] BARCLAY, DAVID BARCLAY OF[1] URIE)[1]* was born August 02, 1988 in Wichita, Sedgwick, Kansas, USA[1]. He married JULIE GOETZ[1] August 10, 2013 in Wichita, Sedgwick, Kansas, USA; Marriage: Eberly Farm[1], daughter of BRAD GOETZ and LINDA. She was born June 14, 1989[1].

Child of AARON BAUDER and JULIE GOETZ is:
- i. ZOEY GRACE[12] BAUDER[1], b. May 15, 2013, Wichita, Sedgwick, Kansas, USA; Wesley Hospital[1].

66. JOSHUA RYAN[11] BAUDER *(CYNTHIA DIANE[10] BEERY, PEGGY JOYCE[9] DURBIN, NELLIE[8] BARKLEY, JOSEPH HENRY LOUIS[7], JAMES M.[6], JAMES M.[5], WILLIAM[4], GEORGE[3], JOHN[2] BARCLAY, DAVID BARCLAY OF[1] URIE)[1]* was born August 24, 1985 in Wichita, Sedgwick, Kansas, USA; Wesley[1]. He married (2) BETHANY KAY LEONARD[1] 2008 in Wichita, Kansas, USA[1]. She was born December 14, 1987[1]. He married (3) TIFFANIE BURTNETT (RAU)[1] January 01, 2013[1], daughter of HAROLD BURTNETT and LAWANA. She was born August 18, 1981[1].

Child of JOSHUA RYAN BAUDER is:
- i. LILA KAY[12] BAUDER[1], b. July 21, 2008, Wichita, Sedgwick, Kansas, USA; Wesley Hospital[1].

Children of JOSHUA BAUDER and TIFFANIE (RAU) are:
- ii. CHEYENNE[12] RAU[1], b. January 19, 2006[1].
- iii. SAMANTHA RAU[1], b. October 25, 2007[1].

67. JILLIAN LEIGH[11] SHELL *(CHERYL DENISE[10] BEERY, PEGGY JOYCE[9] DURBIN, NELLIE[8] BARKLEY, JOSEPH HENRY LOUIS[7], JAMES M.[6], JAMES M.[5], WILLIAM[4], GEORGE[3], JOHN[2] BARCLAY, DAVID BARCLAY OF[1] URIE)[1]* was born December 18, 1989 in Wichita, Sedgwick, Kansas, USA; Wesley Hospital[1]. She married LUIS CARLOS AGRAMONT[1], son of FEDERICO RIVERA and EDITH GUERRA. He was born December 27, 1985 in La Paz, Bolivia, South America[1].

Child of JILLIAN SHELL and LUIS AGRAMONT is:
- i. LEIGHTON[12] AGRAMONT[1], b. June 15, 2014, Frisco, Denton, Texas, USA[1].

Endnotes

1. Barkley_2016-05-03_02.FTW, Date of Import: May 3, 2016.

1   David Barclay of Urie 1610 - 1686
.... +Katherine Gordon
..... 2   David Barclay
..... 2   Jean Barclay
.... +Sir Ewen Cameron
..... 2   John Barclay
.... +Catherine
.... 3   George Barkley 1730 - 1781
.... +Agnes Grant 1732 -
.... 4   John G. Barkley 1750 - 1814
.... 4   John Talbott Barkley 1752 - 1814
.... 4   Hugh Barkley 1760 - 1830
.... +Elizabeth Kirkpatrick 1769 - 1849
.... 5   Margaret Barckley 1788 -
.... 5   Mary Barckley 1789 -
.... +John Cheeseman
.... 5   Jane Barckley 1791 -
.... +Mr. Caldwell
.... *2nd Husband of Jane Barckley:
.... +Andrew McClain
.... 5   Sara Barckley 1791 -
.... +William Clark
.... 5   Martha Barckley 1793 -
.... +John McMillan
.... 5   Elizabeth Barckley 1795 -
.... +Ben Allison
.... 5   William Barckley 1799 -
.... +Polly Allison
.... 5   Ann Barckley 1800 - Infant
.... 5   Andrew Barckley 1801 - 1816
.... 5   Hannah Barckley 1803 -
.... +Alexander Cameron
.... 5   Nancy Kirkpatrick Barckley 1806 -
.... +William Murphy
.... 5   Susannah Barckley 1808 - 1822
.... 5   Hugh Barckley, Jr. 1811 - 1878
.... +Mary Murphy
.... 4   Joseph Barkley 1760 - 1845
.... +Marvilla or Martha 1777 - 1834
.... 5   William Barkley 1791 -
.... 5   Hugh Barkley 1794 - 1860
.... +Ruth Laycock 1804 - 1835
.... 6   Anne Barkley 1816 -
.... +James Houston 1804 -
.... 6   Martha Barkley 1818 - 1863
.... +John Abraham 1766 - 1851
.... 7   Kids Abraham
.... 7   William Milton Abraham 1842 - 1914

```
.....................................  +Eliza Ralston Wayne  1842 - 1927
.....................................  7  Zella Marcella Abraham  1848 -
.....................................  7  Olivia Frances Abraham  1848 -
.....................................  7  Zillah Zeliah Abraham  1851 -
...............................  6  Isaac Barkley  1820 -
...............................  6  Nathan Barkley  1821 - 1865
.....................................  +Sarah Ann Denniston  1829 - 1914
.....................................  7  Fancis M. Barkley  1849 -
.....................................  7  Lorissa B. Barkley  1851 -
.....................................  7  Larisa Belle Barkley  1851 - 1941
.....................................  +Francis Lafayette McDonald  1846 - 1911
.....................................  7  Georgianna Barkley  1855 -
.....................................  7  Charles A. Barkley  1858 -
.....................................  7  Letitia Barkley  1861 -
...............................  6  Margaret Barkley  1821 -
...............................  6  [1] Elizabeth M. Barkley  1830 - 1903
.....................................  +[2] Lewis Carnes  1799 - 1884
.....................................  7  [3] Jesse Luther Carnes  1852 - 1868
.....................................  7  [4] Charles E. Carnes  1854 - 1912
.....................................  +[5] Emma Boys
.....................................  7  [6] Grace Carnes
.....................................  7  [7] Abigail Carnes
.....................................  7  [8] Arthur L. Carnes  1856 -
.....................................  +[9] Florence Donaldson
...............................  6  [10] Franklin Barkley  1834 -
.....................................  +[11] Malinda  1844 -
.....................................  7  [12] Sarah Barkley  1863 -
.....................................  7  [13] Frank Barkley  1869 -
..........................  *2nd Wife of Hugh Barkley:
.............................  +Keziah Donham  1805 - 1851
...............................  6  Nancy Barkley  1827 -
...............................  6  [1] Elizabeth M. Barkley  1830 - 1903
.....................................  +[2] Lewis Carnes  1799 - 1884
.....................................  7  [3] Jesse Luther Carnes  1852 - 1868
.....................................  7  [4] Charles E. Carnes  1854 - 1912
.....................................  +[5] Emma Boys
.....................................  7  [6] Grace Carnes
.....................................  7  [7] Abigail Carnes
.....................................  7  [8] Arthur L. Carnes  1856 -
.....................................  +[9] Florence Donaldson
...............................  6  [10] Franklin Barkley  1834 -
.....................................  +[11] Malinda  1844 -
.....................................  7  [12] Sarah Barkley  1863 -
.....................................  7  [13] Frank Barkley  1869 -
...............................  6  John W. Barkley  1839 -
...............................  6  Enoch Perry Barkley  1841 - 1912
.....................................  +Isabella Grantham  1841 - 1916
.....................................  7  John Elbert Barkley  1863 -
.....................................  +Abbie Foster
.....................................  7  Luther Ellsworth Barkley  1865 - 1940
```

```
.............................................. +Laura Belle McAllister  1867 - 1939
.............................................. 7   William Edgar Barkley  1868 -
.............................................. 7   Charley Walter Barkley  1871 - 1926
.............................................. +Ethel Smith  - 1910
.............................................. *2nd Wife of Charley Walter Barkley:
.............................................. +Ella McLaughlin
.............................................. 7   Ollie Euphemia Barkley  1875 - 1890
.............................................. 7   Laura Dale Barkley  1877 - 1954
.............................................. +Ellis U. Anderson  1872 - 1958
.............................................. 7   Ila Maude Barkley  1879 -
.............................................. +Adrin S. Foster
.............................................. 7   Bertha Bell Barkley  1884 -
.............................................. +Bert Hill  1883 -
......................... 5   Mary Barkley  1794 -
......................... +Benjamin Dugan  1810 - 1870
......................... 5   Sarah Barkley  1794 -
......................... +Elias Thomas
......................... 5   George Barkley  1795 - 1864
......................... +Frances M. Field
............................. 6   George Barkley  1818 - 1857
............................. +Sarah Welch  1820 - 1889
............................. 7   Ann M. Barkley  1845 - 1860
............................. 7   William N. Barkley  1848 - 1870
............................. +Nancy Elizabeth Banta  1855 -
............................. 6   Joseph Barkley  1832 -
............................. 6   John Barkley  1835 -
............................. +Elizabeth Snearly
............................. 6   Emily Barkley  1837 -
............................. +Mr. McCann
............................. 7   Clara McCann
............................. 6   Henry Barkley  1842 -
............................. +Lenora Barron
............................. 6   James Alfred Barkley  1845 -
............................. +Julia A. Clarke
......................... 5   Mary Barkley  1797 -
......................... 5   Andrew Barkley  1799 - 1879
......................... +Elizabeth Ava Merville  1797 - 1879
............................. 6   Amanda Barkley  1829 -
............................. 6   George Washington Barkley  1837 - 1900
............................. +Nancy Wheeten  1834 -
............................. 7   William Henry Barkley  1858 - 1927
............................. +Mabel V. Ellis  1847 - 1966
............................. 8   Willard Henry, Jr. Barkley  1908 - 1976
............................. +Revarlle Bealer  1910 - 1981
............................. 9   Fred William Barkley  1940 - 1996
............................. 10  Randy A. Barkley  1964 - 2002
............................. +Private
............................. 6   Daniel B. Barkley  1841 -
......................... 5   James S. Barkley  1809 -
......................... +Mary Hawkins  1819 -
```

```
.......................... 5   John B. Barkley  1815 - 1931
.............................. +Sarah Clark  1821 - 1864
.............................. 6   Joseph George Barkley  1845 - 1888
.................................. +Josephine Drucilla Metzger  1842 - 1921
.................................. 7   Sarah Jane Barkley  1865 -
...................................... +Hyle Ace Hyde  1841 - 1917
.................................. 7   Rosa E. Barkley  1867 -
...................................... +Brackett Johnson  1847 -
.................................. 7   Lenora E. Barkley  1868 -
...................................... +W. W. Armstrong  1830 - 1904
.................................. 7   Flora C. Barkley  1870 -
...................................... +Ludwig Freidrich Niermann
...................................... *2nd Husband of Flora C. Barkley:
...................................... +LewisNiermann
...................................... *3rd Husband of Flora C. Barkley:
...................................... +David Andrew Miller  1870 -
.................................. 7   Charles Alexander Barkley  1875 -
.................................. 7   John W. Barkley  1877 -
.................................. 7   Silas Barkley  1878 -
.................................. 7   Paul Barkley  1878 - 1925
.................................. 7   William Alfred Barkley  1881 - 1971
.................................. 7   Vida May Barkley  1884 - 1897
.............................. 6   Samuel P. Barkley  1848 -
.................................. +Mary Louise Walken
.................................. 7   Lydia Lillie Barkley  1881 -
...................................... +Frank Drake
.................................. 7   Madie Barkley  1892 -
.............................. 6   Elizabeth J. Barkley  1850 -
.............................. 6   George W. Barkley  1852 - 1931
.................................. +Artensia E. Wilson  1852 - 1929
.................................. 7   George P. Barkley  1876 - 1968
...................................... +Ona Cox
.................................. 7   Mary Ellen Barkley  1878 - 1957
...................................... +Jasper N. Scott  1873 - 1951
.................................. 7   John Gordon Barkley  1889 -
.............................. 6   John William Barkley  1854 - 1921
.................................. +Johanna E. Parson  1862 - 1931
.................................. 7   Vallie Mae Barkley  1879 - 1951
...................................... +Jesse James Kerns
.................................. 7   Ava Lee Barkley  1880 - 1918
...................................... +George Pruitt
.................................. 7   Hanson Barkley  1882 - 1968
...................................... +Maude Turner
.................................. 7   Mary Barkley  1883 - 1883
.................................. 7   Martha Barkley  1883 -
.................................. 7   Alma Jane Barkley  1884 - 1885
.................................. 7   Vida Belle Barkley  1886 - 1890
.................................. 7   Autie William Barkley  1888 - 1919
...................................... +Connie Kerns
.................................. 7   Irby Forest Barkley  1891 - 1969
```

....		+Mima Miller
....	7	Fledda Johanna Barkley 1892 - 1928
....		+Drury Oscar Fairley
....	7	George Elmer Barkley 1894 - 1987
....		+Bessie Raines
....	7	Millard Oda Barkley 1896 - 1918
....	7	Orma Ellen Barkley 1897 - 1988
....		+Wesley Bowers
....	7	Jessie Pearl Barkley 1900 - 1997
....		+Robert Millard Stape
....	7	Charley Barkley 1902 - 1902
....	7	James Roy Barkley 1903 - 1957
....		+Iva Stape
....	6	Martha F. Barkley 1856 -
....	6	Sarah Ellen Barkley 1859 - 1933
....		+John Wiseman Nations 1839 - 1907
....	7	Flora Nations
....	7	Nellie Nations
....	7	Minnie Myrtle Nations 1881 -
....	7	Mary Lucretia Nations 1882 -
....	7	George W. Nations 1887 -
....	7	J. Benjamin Nations 1891 -
....	7	Josephine Pearl Nations 1894 -
....	7	James G. Nations 1896 -
....	6	Thomas J. Barkley 1864 -
....	4	Sarah Barkley 1769 -
....		+John Finley
....	5	Robert Finley
....	5	Levi Finley
....	4	James Barkley 1770 -
....	4	William Barkley 1770 - 1833
....	4	Thomas Barkley 1777 -
....	4	William Barkley 1774 - 1833
....		+Rebecca Newkirk 1774 - 1834
....	5	James M. Barkley 1795 - 1830
....		+Elizabeth Carter 1801 - 1878
....	6	William G. Barkley 1820 - 1900
....		+Charlotte Norris 1827 -
....	7	Melissa J. Barkley 1844 -
....	7	Mary C. Barkley 1850 -
....	7	Rebecca Ellen Barkley 1852 -
....	7	William P. Barkley 1857 -
....	7	George Barkley 1861 -
....	6	Catherine Ella Barkley 1822 - 1884
....		+James C. Cooper - 1869
....	7	Elizabeth Rebecca Cooper 1840 -
....	7	Mary Ellen Cooper 1841 -
....	7	Maria Jane Cooper 1845 -
....	7	Louisa Malvina Cooper 1848 -
....	7	William Cooper 1854 -

.... 7   James Perry Cooper 1861 -
.... 7   Charles Cooper 1863 -
.... *2nd Husband of Catherine Ella Barkley:
.... +David Steelman
.... 6   Perry Henry Barkley 1824 - 1886
.... +Mary Mae Stillman 1826 - 1907
.... 7   David H. Barkley 1847 -
.... 7   James W. Barkley 1848 - 1928
.... 7   [108] Joseph Henry Louis Barkley 1852 - 1931
.... +[109] Mary Elizabeth Barber 1862 - 1930
.... 8   [110] Rena B. Barkley 1882 - 1935
.... 8   [111] Stella Mae Barkley 1884 - 1971
.... +[112] Orris Estes
.... *2nd Husband of [111] Stella Mae Barkley:
.... +[113] Cal Chastain
.... 9   [114] Calvin Chastain, Jr.
.... 8   [115] Oren Perry Barkley 1886 - 1959
.... 8   [116] Josephine Edna Barkley 1888 - 1932
.... +[117] Joe Minarick
.... 8   [118] Arthur Harrison Barkley 1889 - 1974
.... +[119] Mary Aletha Steele
.... 9   [120] Harry Arthur Barkley
.... +[121] Margaret Douglas
.... 10   [122] Steve Barkley
.... 10   [14] Robert Louis Barkley
.... +[15] Anna May
.... 11   [16] Kenny Barkley
.... 11   [17] Bradley Barkley
.... 9   [14] Robert Louis Barkley
.... +[15] Anna May
.... 10   [16] Kenny Barkley
.... 10   [17] Bradley Barkley
.... 8   [123] Elizabeth Jay Barkley 1893 - 1975
.... +[124] Harry Beaufort
.... 9   [125] Harry Beaufort, Jr.
.... 9   [126] Dorothy Beaufort 1920 -
.... +[127] Spivey
.... 10   [128] Keith Douglas Spivey 1948 -
.... 10   [129] Glynn Lyneau Spivey 1951 -
.... *2nd Husband of [126] Dorothy Beaufort:
.... +[130] Kelly
.... 9   [131] Robert Lewis Beaufort
.... +[132] Fairy - 1977
.... 10   [133] Galen Beaufort
.... 10   [134] Becky Beaufort
.... 8   [135] Alma Myrtle Barkley 1895 - 1988
.... +[136] Arthur Kirkner 1881 - 1921
.... 8   [137] Marion Harvey Barkley 1898 -
.... +[138] Ruby Moberly
.... 8   [139] Nellie Barkley 1900 - 1948

.... +[19] Ufa Henry Durbin 1899 - 1958
.... 9 [20] Marvin Darrell Durbin 1924 - 1992
.... +[21] Susan Mae Webster 1946 -
.... 10 [22] Victoria Lynn Durbin 1966 -
.... 10 [23] Tamara Sue Durbin 1974 -
.... *2nd Wife of [20] Marvin Darrell Durbin:
.... +[24] Joan LaDuke
.... 10 [25] Donna Rae LaDuke 1957 -
.... 10 [26] Richard Lee LaDuke 1960 -
.... *3rd Wife of [20] Marvin Darrell Durbin:
.... +[27] Betty Lee Schmidt
.... 10 [28] Darrell Lee Durbin 1948 -
.... 10 [29] Carolyn Sue Durbin 1949 - 1957
.... 10 [30] David Lawrence Durbin - 1996
.... 9 [31] Jack Calvin Durbin 1925 - 2012
.... +[32] Mae Dean Wooley 1928 - 2010
.... 10 [33] Dorothy Annette Durbin 1955 - 1955
.... 10 [34] Debra Jeanette Durbin 1955 -
.... 10 [35] Blake Calvin Durbin 1967 -
.... 9 [36] Leonard Leroy Durbin 1927 - 1995
.... 9 [37] Betty Jewell Durbin 1931 -
.... +[38] Winfred Lee Carson, Sr. 1920 - 1991
.... 10 [39] Winfred Lee Carson, Jr. 1954 -
.... +[40] Sanda Kandi 1946 -
.... 11 [41] Terrance Dale Carson 1979 -
.... +[42] Dionne Petersen
.... 12 [43] Tyler Dale Carson 1999 -
.... 12 [44] Taylor Nichole Carson 2002 -
.... 12 [45] Tiffanie Jean Carson 2002 -
.... 11 [46] Jason Lee Carson 1981 -
.... 11 [47] Nicole Neela Carson 1988 -
.... 10 [48] Bonnie Lee Carson 1957 -
.... +[49] Robert William Johnson
.... *2nd Husband of [48] Bonnie Lee Carson:
.... +[50] Kevin Lee Peck
.... *3rd Husband of [48] Bonnie Lee Carson:
.... +[51] Daniel Miller
.... 11 [52] Daniel Lee Miller 2000 -
.... 9 [53] Doris May Durbin 1932 - 2014
.... +[54] Ovid Maurice Wooley 1933 - 2004
.... 10 [55] Martha Ann Wooley 1953 -
.... +[56] Paul John Barthelome Volcherick
.... 11 [57] Lane Edward Volcherick 1980 -
.... 10 [58] Ovid Maurice Wooley, Jr. 1955 -
.... 10 [59] Richard Lynn Wooley 1959 -
.... +[60] Brenda Kay Miller 1961 -
.... 11 [61] Jason Neil Wooley 1976 -
.... 11 [62] Kaveh Marlin Wooley 1978 -
.... 11 [63] Kapril Michelle Wooley 1987 -
.... *2nd Wife of [59] Richard Lynn Wooley:

```
................................................ +[64] Rhonda Robberson
................................................ 11 [65] Larry Robberson  1977 -
.......................................... 10 [66] Beverly Sue Wooley  1962 -
.......................................... 10 [67] Peggy Jean Wooley  1964 -
................................................ +[68] Ricky Dean Shawback
................................................ 11 [69] Peggy LeeAnn Shawback  1984 -
................................................ 11 [70] Chrystal May Shawback  1986 -
................................................ 11 [71] Lauane Marrie Shawback  1988 -
.................................... 9  [72] Peggy Joyce Durbin  1936 -
.......................................... +[73] Irvin Lee Beery  1934 - 2012
.......................................... 10 [74] Vicki Lynn Beery  1956 -
................................................ +[75] Jerry Allan Smith  1954 -
................................................ 11 [76] Andrew Philip Smith  1985 -
................................................ 11 [77] Anna Elizabeth Smith  1987 -
...................................................... +[78] Noah Daniel McLaughlin  1984 -
...................................................... 12 [79] Harley Lyne McLaughlin  2009 -
...................................................... 12 [80] Tristin Robert Lee McLaughlin  2011 -
                                                            2011
...................................................... 12 [81] Rustin Rae McLaughlin  2011 -
...................................................... 12 [82] Hope Elizabeth McLaughlin  2012 -
................................................ 11 [83] Lydia Abigail Smith  1991 -
...................................................... +[84] Aaron Cress  1991 -
................................................ 11 [85] Leah Rachel Smith  1992 -
.......................................... 10 [86] Cynthia Diane Beery  1958 -
................................................ +[87] Karl Warren Bauder  1954 -
................................................ 11 [88] Aaron Thomas Bauder  1988 -
...................................................... +[89] Julie Goetz  1989 -
...................................................... 12 [90] Zoey Grace Bauder  2013 -
................................................ 11 [91] Joshua Ryan Bauder  1985 -
...................................................... 12 [18] Lila Kay Bauder  2008 -
...................................................... +[92] Bethany Kay Leonard  1987 -
...................................................... 12 [18] Lila Kay Bauder  2008 -
................................................ *2nd Wife of [91] Joshua Ryan Bauder:
...................................................... +[93] Tiffanie Burtnett (Rau)  1981 -
...................................................... 12 [94] Cheyenne Rau  2006 -
...................................................... 12 [95] Samantha Rau  2007 -
.......................................... 10 [96] Cheryl Denise Beery  1963 -
................................................ +[97] Larry Philip Shell Jr.  1962 -
................................................ 11 [98] Lauren Ashley Shell  1987 -
................................................ 11 [99] Jillian Leigh Shell  1989 -
...................................................... +[100] Luis Carlos Agramont  1985 -
...................................................... 12 [101] Leighton Agramont  2014 -
.......................................... *2nd Husband of [96] Cheryl Denise Beery:
.................................................... +[102] Dick Aldes Holihan Jr.  1956 -
.................................... 9  [103] Carol Jean Durbin  1940 -
.......................................... +[104] Arthur Bidner  1932 -
.......................................... 10 [105] Susan Jeanette Bidner  1963 -
................................................ +[106] James Edward Burns  1964 -
................................................ 11 [107] Benjamin Alexander Burns  2002 -
.......................................... 8  [140] Berniece Naomi Barkley  1902 - 1989
```

+[141] Bruce Adams
8 [142] Nellie Barkley 1900 - 1948
+[19] Ufa Henry Durbin 1899 - 1958
9 [20] Marvin Darrell Durbin 1924 - 1992
+[21] Susan Mae Webster 1946 -
10 [22] Victoria Lynn Durbin 1966 -
10 [23] Tamara Sue Durbin 1974 -
*2nd Wife of [20] Marvin Darrell Durbin:
+[24] Joan LaDuke
10 [25] Donna Rae LaDuke 1957 -
10 [26] Richard Lee LaDuke 1960 -
*3rd Wife of [20] Marvin Darrell Durbin:
+[27] Betty Lee Schmidt
10 [28] Darrell Lee Durbin 1948 -
10 [29] Carolyn Sue Durbin 1949 - 1957
10 [30] David Lawrence Durbin - 1996
9 [31] Jack Calvin Durbin 1925 - 2012
+[32] Mae Dean Wooley 1928 - 2010
10 [33] Dorothy Annette Durbin 1955 - 1955
10 [34] Debra Jeanette Durbin 1955 -
10 [35] Blake Calvin Durbin 1967 -
9 [36] Leonard Leroy Durbin 1927 - 1995
9 [37] Betty Jewell Durbin 1931 -
+[38] Winfred Lee Carson, Sr. 1920 - 1991
10 [39] Winfred Lee Carson, Jr. 1954 -
+[40] Sanda Kandi 1946 -
11 [41] Terrance Dale Carson 1979 -
+[42] Dionne Petersen
12 [43] Tyler Dale Carson 1999 -
12 [44] Taylor Nichole Carson 2002 -
12 [45] Tiffanie Jean Carson 2002 -
11 [46] Jason Lee Carson 1981 -
11 [47] Nicole Neela Carson 1988 -
10 [48] Bonnie Lee Carson 1957 -
+[49] Robert William Johnson
*2nd Husband of [48] Bonnie Lee Carson:
+[50] Kevin Lee Peck
*3rd Husband of [48] Bonnie Lee Carson:
+[51] Daniel Miller
11 [52] Daniel Lee Miller 2000 -
9 [53] Doris May Durbin 1932 - 2014
+[54] Ovid Maurice Wooley 1933 - 2004
10 [55] Martha Ann Wooley 1953 -
+[56] Paul John Barthelome Volcherick
11 [57] Lane Edward Volcherick 1980 -
10 [58] Ovid Maurice Wooley, Jr. 1955 -
10 [59] Richard Lynn Wooley 1959 -
+[60] Brenda Kay Miller 1961 -
11 [61] Jason Neil Wooley 1976 -
11 [62] Kaveh Marlin Wooley 1978 -

```
................................................ 11  [63] Kapril Michelle Wooley  1987 -
................................................ *2nd Wife of [59] Richard Lynn Wooley:
................................................  +[64] Rhonda Robberson
................................................ 11  [65] Larry Robberson  1977 -
................................................ 10  [66] Beverly Sue Wooley  1962 -
................................................ 10  [67] Peggy Jean Wooley  1964 -
................................................  +[68] Ricky Dean Shawback
................................................ 11  [69] Peggy LeeAnn Shawback  1984 -
................................................ 11  [70] Chrystal May Shawback  1986 -
................................................ 11  [71] Lauane Marrie Shawback  1988 -
................................................  9  [72] Peggy Joyce Durbin  1936 -
................................................  +[73] Irvin Lee Beery  1934 - 2012
................................................ 10  [74] Vicki Lynn Beery  1956 -
................................................  +[75] Jerry Allan Smith  1954 -
................................................ 11  [76] Andrew Philip Smith  1985 -
................................................ 11  [77] Anna Elizabeth Smith  1987 -
................................................  +[78] Noah Daniel McLaughlin  1984 -
................................................ 12  [79] Harley Lyne McLaughlin  2009 -
................................................ 12  [80] Tristin Robert Lee McLaughlin  2011 -
                                                      2011
................................................ 12  [81] Rustin Rae McLaughlin  2011 -
................................................ 12  [82] Hope Elizabeth McLaughlin  2012 -
................................................ 11  [83] Lydia Abigail Smith  1991 -
................................................  +[84] Aaron Cress  1991 -
................................................ 11  [85] Leah Rachel Smith  1992 -
................................................ 10  [86] Cynthia Diane Beery  1958 -
................................................  +[87] Karl Warren Bauder  1954 -
................................................ 11  [88] Aaron Thomas Bauder  1988 -
................................................  +[89] Julie Goetz  1989 -
................................................ 12  [90] Zoey Grace Bauder  2013 -
................................................ 11  [91] Joshua Ryan Bauder  1985 -
................................................ 12  [18] Lila Kay Bauder  2008 -
................................................  +[92] Bethany Kay Leonard  1987 -
................................................ 12  [18] Lila Kay Bauder  2008 -
................................................ *2nd Wife of [91] Joshua Ryan Bauder:
................................................  +[93] Tiffanie Burtnett (Rau)  1981 -
................................................ 12  [94] Cheyenne Rau  2006 -
................................................ 12  [95] Samantha Rau  2007 -
................................................ 10  [96] Cheryl Denise Beery  1963 -
................................................  +[97] Larry Philip Shell Jr.  1962 -
................................................ 11  [98] Lauren Ashley Shell  1987 -
................................................ 11  [99] Jillian Leigh Shell  1989 -
................................................  +[100] Luis Carlos Agramont  1985 -
................................................ 12  [101] Leighton Agramont  2014 -
................................................ *2nd Husband of [96] Cheryl Denise Beery:
................................................  +[102] Dick Aldes Holihan Jr.  1956 -
................................................  9  [103] Carol Jean Durbin  1940 -
................................................  +[104] Arthur Bidner  1932 -
................................................ 10  [105] Susan Jeanette Bidner  1963 -
................................................  +[106] James Edward Burns  1964 -
```

```
.......................................... 11  [107] Benjamin Alexander Burns  2002 -
.......................................  7   Theodore William Barkley  1853 - 1926
..........................................      +Rosella Amanda Mounts  1871 - 1956
.......................................  7   Asa Tell Barkley  1856 -
..........................................      +Elizabeth Fritz
.......................................  7   Hosea Stillman Barkley  1859 - 1946
..........................................      +Julia Enos Mounts
.......................................  7   Ida Barkley  1861 -
.......................................  7   Charles C. Barkley  1866 - 1941
...............................  6   Rebecca Emeline Barkley  1826 - 1897
..........................................      +James Corbin  1817 - 1891
...............................  6   Henry Carter Barkley  1827 - 1892
...............................          +Melissa Bushman  1840 - 1927
.......................................  7   Clarence Barkley  1876 -
.......................................  7   George Curtis Barkley  1871 -
...............................  *2nd Wife of Henry Carter Barkley:
...............................          +Barbara Jane Clarke  1832 -
.......................................  7   John Spencer Barkley  1852 -
.......................................  7   Mary Ida Barkley  1860 -
.......................................  7   Ella Carter Barkley  1867 -
.......................................  7   George Curtis Barkley  1871 -
.......................................  7   Maria Belle Barkley  1857 -
.......................................  7   Sarah Jane Barkley  1863 -
...............................  6   James M. Barkley  1831 - 1851
...............................          +Elizabeth Richards  1833 -
.......................................  7   [108] Joseph Henry Louis Barkley  1852 - 1931
..........................................      +[109] Mary Elizabeth Barber  1862 - 1930
..........................................  8   [110] Rena B. Barkley  1882 - 1935
..........................................  8   [111] Stella Mae Barkley  1884 - 1971
..........................................      +[112] Orris Estes
..........................................  *2nd Husband of [111] Stella Mae Barkley:
..........................................      +[113] Cal Chastain
.............................................  9   [114] Calvin Chastain, Jr.
..........................................  8   [115] Oren Perry Barkley  1886 - 1959
..........................................  8   [116] Josephine Edna Barkley  1888 - 1932
..........................................      +[117] Joe Minarick
..........................................  8   [118] Arthur Harrison Barkley  1889 - 1974
..........................................      +[119] Mary Aletha Steele
.............................................  9   [120] Harry Arthur Barkley
.................................................      +[121] Margaret Douglas
.................................................  10  [122] Steve Barkley
.................................................  10  [14] Robert Louis Barkley
.................................................      +[15] Anna May
....................................................  11  [16] Kenny Barkley
....................................................  11  [17] Bradley Barkley
.............................................  9   [14] Robert Louis Barkley
.............................................      +[15] Anna May
.............................................  10  [16] Kenny Barkley
.............................................  10  [17] Bradley Barkley
..........................................  8   [123] Elizabeth Jay Barkley  1893 - 1975
```

```
.................................... +[124] Harry Beaufort
.................................... 9  [125] Harry Beaufort, Jr.
.................................... 9  [126] Dorothy Beaufort  1920 -
....................................    +[127] Spivey
....................................     10 [128] Keith Douglas Spivey  1948 -
....................................     10 [129] Glynn Lyneau Spivey  1951 -
.................................... *2nd Husband of [126] Dorothy Beaufort:
....................................    +[130] Kelly
.................................... 9  [131] Robert Lewis Beaufort
....................................    +[132] Fairy - 1977
....................................     10 [133] Galen Beaufort
....................................     10 [134] Becky Beaufort
.................................... 8  [135] Alma Myrtle Barkley  1895 - 1988
....................................    +[136] Arthur Kirkner  1881 - 1921
.................................... 8  [137] Marion Harvey Barkley  1898 -
....................................    +[138] Ruby Moberly
.................................... 8  [139] Nellie Barkley  1900 - 1948
....................................    +[19] Ufa Henry Durbin  1899 - 1958
.................................... 9  [20] Marvin Darrell Durbin  1924 - 1992
....................................    +[21] Susan Mae Webster  1946 -
....................................     10 [22] Victoria Lynn Durbin  1966 -
....................................     10 [23] Tamara Sue Durbin  1974 -
.................................... *2nd Wife of [20] Marvin Darrell Durbin:
....................................    +[24] Joan LaDuke
....................................     10 [25] Donna Rae LaDuke  1957 -
....................................     10 [26] Richard Lee LaDuke  1960 -
.................................... *3rd Wife of [20] Marvin Darrell Durbin:
....................................    +[27] Betty Lee Schmidt
....................................     10 [28] Darrell Lee Durbin  1948 -
....................................     10 [29] Carolyn Sue Durbin  1949 - 1957
....................................     10 [30] David Lawrence Durbin  - 1996
.................................... 9  [31] Jack Calvin Durbin  1925 - 2012
....................................    +[32] Mae Dean Wooley  1928 - 2010
....................................     10 [33] Dorothy Annette Durbin  1955 - 1955
....................................     10 [34] Debra Jeanette Durbin  1955 -
....................................     10 [35] Blake Calvin Durbin  1967 -
.................................... 9  [36] Leonard Leroy Durbin  1927 - 1995
.................................... 9  [37] Betty Jewell Durbin  1931 -
....................................    +[38] Winfred Lee Carson, Sr.  1920 - 1991
....................................     10 [39] Winfred Lee Carson, Jr.  1954 -
....................................       +[40] Sanda Kandi  1946 -
....................................        11 [41] Terrance Dale Carson  1979 -
....................................          +[42] Dionne Petersen
....................................           12 [43] Tyler Dale Carson  1999 -
....................................           12 [44] Taylor Nichole Carson  2002 -
....................................           12 [45] Tiffanie Jean Carson  2002 -
....................................        11 [46] Jason Lee Carson  1981 -
....................................        11 [47] Nicole Neela Carson  1988 -
....................................     10 [48] Bonnie Lee Carson  1957 -
....................................       +[49] Robert William Johnson
```

.... *2nd Husband of [48] Bonnie Lee Carson:
.... +[50] Kevin Lee Peck
.... *3rd Husband of [48] Bonnie Lee Carson:
.... +[51] Daniel Miller
.... 11 [52] Daniel Lee Miller 2000 -
.... 9 [53] Doris May Durbin 1932 - 2014
.... +[54] Ovid Maurice Wooley 1933 - 2004
.... 10 [55] Martha Ann Wooley 1953 -
.... +[56] Paul John Barthelome Volcherick
.... 11 [57] Lane Edward Volcherick 1980 -
.... 10 [58] Ovid Maurice Wooley, Jr. 1955 -
.... 10 [59] Richard Lynn Wooley 1959 -
.... +[60] Brenda Kay Miller 1961 -
.... 11 [61] Jason Neil Wooley 1976 -
.... 11 [62] Kaveh Marlin Wooley 1978 -
.... 11 [63] Kapril Michelle Wooley 1987 -
.... *2nd Wife of [59] Richard Lynn Wooley:
.... +[64] Rhonda Robberson
.... 11 [65] Larry Robberson 1977 -
.... 10 [66] Beverly Sue Wooley 1962 -
.... 10 [67] Peggy Jean Wooley 1964 -
.... +[68] Ricky Dean Shawback
.... 11 [69] Peggy LeeAnn Shawback 1984 -
.... 11 [70] Chrystal May Shawback 1986 -
.... 11 [71] Lauane Marrie Shawback 1988 -
.... 9 [72] Peggy Joyce Durbin 1936 -
.... +[73] Irvin Lee Beery 1934 - 2012
.... 10 [74] Vicki Lynn Beery 1956 -
.... +[75] Jerry Allan Smith 1954 -
.... 11 [76] Andrew Philip Smith 1985 -
.... 11 [77] Anna Elizabeth Smith 1987 -
.... +[78] Noah Daniel McLaughlin 1984 -
.... 12 [79] Harley Lyne McLaughlin 2009 -
.... 12 [80] Tristin Robert Lee McLaughlin 2011 - 2011
.... 12 [81] Rustin Rae McLaughlin 2011 -
.... 12 [82] Hope Elizabeth McLaughlin 2012 -
.... 11 [83] Lydia Abigail Smith 1991 -
.... +[84] Aaron Cress 1991 -
.... 11 [85] Leah Rachel Smith 1992 -
.... 10 [86] Cynthia Diane Beery 1958 -
.... +[87] Karl Warren Bauder 1954 -
.... 11 [88] Aaron Thomas Bauder 1988 -
.... +[89] Julie Goetz 1989 -
.... 12 [90] Zoey Grace Bauder 2013 -
.... 11 [91] Joshua Ryan Bauder 1985 -
.... 12 [18] Lila Kay Bauder 2008 -
.... +[92] Bethany Kay Leonard 1987 -
.... 12 [18] Lila Kay Bauder 2008 -
.... *2nd Wife of [91] Joshua Ryan Bauder:

+[93] Tiffanie Burtnett (Rau) 1981 -
12 [94] Cheyenne Rau 2006 -
12 [95] Samantha Rau 2007 -
10 [96] Cheryl Denise Beery 1963 -
+[97] Larry Philip Shell Jr. 1962 -
11 [98] Lauren Ashley Shell 1987 -
11 [99] Jillian Leigh Shell 1989 -
+[100] Luis Carlos Agramont 1985 -
12 [101] Leighton Agramont 2014 -
*2nd Husband of [96] Cheryl Denise Beery:
+[102] Dick Aldes Holihan Jr. 1956 -
9   [103] Carol Jean Durbin 1940 -
+[104] Arthur Bidner 1932 -
10 [105] Susan Jeanette Bidner 1963 -
+[106] James Edward Burns 1964 -
11 [107] Benjamin Alexander Burns 2002 -
8   [140] Berniece Naomi Barkley 1902 - 1989
+[141] Bruce Adams
8   [142] Nellie Barkley 1900 - 1948
+[19] Ufa Henry Durbin 1899 - 1958
9   [20] Marvin Darrell Durbin 1924 - 1992
+[21] Susan Mae Webster 1946 -
10 [22] Victoria Lynn Durbin 1966 -
10 [23] Tamara Sue Durbin 1974 -
*2nd Wife of [20] Marvin Darrell Durbin:
+[24] Joan LaDuke
10 [25] Donna Rae LaDuke 1957 -
10 [26] Richard Lee LaDuke 1960 -
*3rd Wife of [20] Marvin Darrell Durbin:
+[27] Betty Lee Schmidt
10 [28] Darrell Lee Durbin 1948 -
10 [29] Carolyn Sue Durbin 1949 - 1957
10 [30] David Lawrence Durbin - 1996
9   [31] Jack Calvin Durbin 1925 - 2012
+[32] Mae Dean Wooley 1928 - 2010
10 [33] Dorothy Annette Durbin 1955 - 1955
10 [34] Debra Jeanette Durbin 1955 -
10 [35] Blake Calvin Durbin 1967 -
9   [36] Leonard Leroy Durbin 1927 - 1995
9   [37] Betty Jewell Durbin 1931 -
+[38] Winfred Lee Carson, Sr. 1920 - 1991
10 [39] Winfred Lee Carson, Jr. 1954 -
+[40] Sanda Kandi 1946 -
11 [41] Terrance Dale Carson 1979 -
+[42] Dionne Petersen
12 [43] Tyler Dale Carson 1999 -
12 [44] Taylor Nichole Carson 2002 -
12 [45] Tiffanie Jean Carson 2002 -
11 [46] Jason Lee Carson 1981 -
11 [47] Nicole Neela Carson 1988 -

.... 10 [48] Bonnie Lee Carson 1957 -
.... +[49] Robert William Johnson
.... *2nd Husband of [48] Bonnie Lee Carson:
.... +[50] Kevin Lee Peck
.... *3rd Husband of [48] Bonnie Lee Carson:
.... +[51] Daniel Miller
.... 11 [52] Daniel Lee Miller 2000 -
.... 9 [53] Doris May Durbin 1932 - 2014
.... +[54] Ovid Maurice Wooley 1933 - 2004
.... 10 [55] Martha Ann Wooley 1953 -
.... +[56] Paul John Barthelome Volcherick
.... 11 [57] Lane Edward Volcherick 1980 -
.... 10 [58] Ovid Maurice Wooley, Jr. 1955 -
.... 10 [59] Richard Lynn Wooley 1959 -
.... +[60] Brenda Kay Miller 1961 -
.... 11 [61] Jason Neil Wooley 1976 -
.... 11 [62] Kaveh Marlin Wooley 1978 -
.... 11 [63] Kapril Michelle Wooley 1987 -
.... *2nd Wife of [59] Richard Lynn Wooley:
.... +[64] Rhonda Robberson
.... 11 [65] Larry Robberson 1977 -
.... 10 [66] Beverly Sue Wooley 1962 -
.... 10 [67] Peggy Jean Wooley 1964 -
.... +[68] Ricky Dean Shawback
.... 11 [69] Peggy LeeAnn Shawback 1984 -
.... 11 [70] Chrystal May Shawback 1986 -
.... 11 [71] Lauane Marrie Shawback 1988 -
.... 9 [72] Peggy Joyce Durbin 1936 -
.... +[73] Irvin Lee Beery 1934 - 2012
.... 10 [74] Vicki Lynn Beery 1956 -
.... +[75] Jerry Allan Smith 1954 -
.... 11 [76] Andrew Philip Smith 1985 -
.... 11 [77] Anna Elizabeth Smith 1987 -
.... +[78] Noah Daniel McLaughlin 1984 -
.... 12 [79] Harley Lyne McLaughlin 2009 -
.... 12 [80] Tristin Robert Lee McLaughlin 2011 -
2011
.... 12 [81] Rustin Rae McLaughlin 2011 -
.... 12 [82] Hope Elizabeth McLaughlin 2012 -
.... 11 [83] Lydia Abigail Smith 1991 -
.... +[84] Aaron Cress 1991 -
.... 11 [85] Leah Rachel Smith 1992 -
.... 10 [86] Cynthia Diane Beery 1958 -
.... +[87] Karl Warren Bauder 1954 -
.... 11 [88] Aaron Thomas Bauder 1988 -
.... +[89] Julie Goetz 1989 -
.... 12 [90] Zoey Grace Bauder 2013 -
.... 11 [91] Joshua Ryan Bauder 1985 -
.... 12 [18] Lila Kay Bauder 2008 -
.... +[92] Bethany Kay Leonard 1987 -

```
................................................ 12 [18] Lila Kay Bauder  2008 -
................................................ *2nd Wife of [91] Joshua Ryan Bauder:
................................................ +[93] Tiffanie Burtnett (Rau)  1981 -
................................................ 12 [94] Cheyenne Rau  2006 -
................................................ 12 [95] Samantha Rau  2007 -
................................................ 10 [96] Cheryl Denise Beery  1963 -
................................................ +[97] Larry Philip Shell Jr.  1962 -
................................................ 11 [98] Lauren Ashley Shell  1987 -
................................................ 11 [99] Jillian Leigh Shell  1989 -
................................................ +[100] Luis Carlos Agramont  1985 -
................................................ 12 [101] Leighton Agramont  2014 -
................................................ *2nd Husband of [96] Cheryl Denise Beery:
................................................ +[102] Dick Aldes Holihan Jr.  1956 -
................................................ 9  [103] Carol Jean Durbin  1940 -
................................................ +[104] Arthur Bidner  1932 -
................................................ 10 [105] Susan Jeanette Bidner  1963 -
................................................ +[106] James Edward Burns  1964 -
................................................ 11 [107] Benjamin Alexander Burns  2002 -
................................................ 7  Oliver G. Barkley  1854 -
................................................ 7  Wilhelmina Jane "Mina" Barkley  1857 - 1935
................................................ 7  Sarah B. Barkley  1860 -
................................................ 7  James Barkley  1862 -
................................................ *2nd Wife of James M. Barkley:
................................................ +Elizabeth/Evelyn Richards  1827 - 1861
................................................ 7  [108] Joseph Henry Louis Barkley  1852 - 1931
................................................ +[109] Mary Elizabeth Barber  1862 - 1930
................................................ 8  [110] Rena B. Barkley  1882 - 1935
................................................ 8  [111] Stella Mae Barkley  1884 - 1971
................................................ +[112] Orris Estes
................................................ *2nd Husband of [111] Stella Mae Barkley:
................................................ +[113] Cal Chastain
................................................ 9  [114] Calvin Chastain, Jr.
................................................ 8  [115] Oren Perry Barkley  1886 - 1959
................................................ 8  [116] Josephine Edna Barkley  1888 - 1932
................................................ +[117] Joe Minarick
................................................ 8  [118] Arthur Harrison Barkley  1889 - 1974
................................................ +[119] Mary Aletha Steele
................................................ 9  [120] Harry Arthur Barkley
................................................ +[121] Margaret Douglas
................................................ 10 [122] Steve Barkley
................................................ 10 [14] Robert Louis Barkley
................................................ +[15] Anna May
................................................ 11 [16] Kenny Barkley
................................................ 11 [17] Bradley Barkley
................................................ 9  [14] Robert Louis Barkley
................................................ +[15] Anna May
................................................ 10 [16] Kenny Barkley
................................................ 10 [17] Bradley Barkley
................................................ 8  [123] Elizabeth Jay Barkley  1893 - 1975
................................................ +[124] Harry Beaufort
```

.... 9 [125] Harry Beaufort, Jr.
.... 9 [126] Dorothy Beaufort 1920 -
.... +[127] Spivey
.... 10 [128] Keith Douglas Spivey 1948 -
.... 10 [129] Glynn Lyneau Spivey 1951 -
.... *2nd Husband of [126] Dorothy Beaufort:
.... +[130] Kelly
.... 9 [131] Robert Lewis Beaufort
.... +[132] Fairy - 1977
.... 10 [133] Galen Beaufort
.... 10 [134] Becky Beaufort
.... 8 [135] Alma Myrtle Barkley 1895 - 1988
.... +[136] Arthur Kirkner 1881 - 1921
.... 8 [137] Marion Harvey Barkley 1898 -
.... +[138] Ruby Moberly
.... 8 [139] Nellie Barkley 1900 - 1948
.... +[19] Ufa Henry Durbin 1899 - 1958
.... 9 [20] Marvin Darrell Durbin 1924 - 1992
.... +[21] Susan Mae Webster 1946 -
.... 10 [22] Victoria Lynn Durbin 1966 -
.... 10 [23] Tamara Sue Durbin 1974 -
.... *2nd Wife of [20] Marvin Darrell Durbin:
.... +[24] Joan LaDuke
.... 10 [25] Donna Rae LaDuke 1957 -
.... 10 [26] Richard Lee LaDuke 1960 -
.... *3rd Wife of [20] Marvin Darrell Durbin:
.... +[27] Betty Lee Schmidt
.... 10 [28] Darrell Lee Durbin 1948 -
.... 10 [29] Carolyn Sue Durbin 1949 - 1957
.... 10 [30] David Lawrence Durbin - 1996
.... 9 [31] Jack Calvin Durbin 1925 - 2012
.... +[32] Mae Dean Wooley 1928 - 2010
.... 10 [33] Dorothy Annette Durbin 1955 - 1955
.... 10 [34] Debra Jeanette Durbin 1955 -
.... 10 [35] Blake Calvin Durbin 1967 -
.... 9 [36] Leonard Leroy Durbin 1927 - 1995
.... 9 [37] Betty Jewell Durbin 1931 -
.... +[38] Winfred Lee Carson, Sr. 1920 - 1991
.... 10 [39] Winfred Lee Carson, Jr. 1954 -
.... +[40] Sanda Kandi 1946 -
.... 11 [41] Terrance Dale Carson 1979 -
.... +[42] Dionne Petersen
.... 12 [43] Tyler Dale Carson 1999 -
.... 12 [44] Taylor Nichole Carson 2002 -
.... 12 [45] Tiffanie Jean Carson 2002 -
.... 11 [46] Jason Lee Carson 1981 -
.... 11 [47] Nicole Neela Carson 1988 -
.... 10 [48] Bonnie Lee Carson 1957 -
.... +[49] Robert William Johnson
.... *2nd Husband of [48] Bonnie Lee Carson:

.... +[50] Kevin Lee Peck
.... *3rd Husband of [48] Bonnie Lee Carson:
.... +[51] Daniel Miller
.... 11 [52] Daniel Lee Miller 2000 -
.... 9 [53] Doris May Durbin 1932 - 2014
.... +[54] Ovid Maurice Wooley 1933 - 2004
.... 10 [55] Martha Ann Wooley 1953 -
.... +[56] Paul John Barthelome Volcherick
.... 11 [57] Lane Edward Volcherick 1980 -
.... 10 [58] Ovid Maurice Wooley, Jr. 1955 -
.... 10 [59] Richard Lynn Wooley 1959 -
.... +[60] Brenda Kay Miller 1961 -
.... 11 [61] Jason Neil Wooley 1976 -
.... 11 [62] Kaveh Marlin Wooley 1978 -
.... 11 [63] Kapril Michelle Wooley 1987 -
.... *2nd Wife of [59] Richard Lynn Wooley:
.... +[64] Rhonda Robberson
.... 11 [65] Larry Robberson 1977 -
.... 10 [66] Beverly Sue Wooley 1962 -
.... 10 [67] Peggy Jean Wooley 1964 -
.... +[68] Ricky Dean Shawback
.... 11 [69] Peggy LeeAnn Shawback 1984 -
.... 11 [70] Chrystal May Shawback 1986 -
.... 11 [71] Lauane Marrie Shawback 1988 -
.... 9 [72] Peggy Joyce Durbin 1936 -
.... +[73] Irvin Lee Beery 1934 - 2012
.... 10 [74] Vicki Lynn Beery 1956 -
.... +[75] Jerry Allan Smith 1954 -
.... 11 [76] Andrew Philip Smith 1985 -
.... 11 [77] Anna Elizabeth Smith 1987 -
.... +[78] Noah Daniel McLaughlin 1984 -
.... 12 [79] Harley Lyne McLaughlin 2009 -
.... 12 [80] Tristin Robert Lee McLaughlin 2011 -
         2011
.... 12 [81] Rustin Rae McLaughlin 2011 -
.... 12 [82] Hope Elizabeth McLaughlin 2012 -
.... 11 [83] Lydia Abigail Smith 1991 -
.... +[84] Aaron Cress 1991 -
.... 11 [85] Leah Rachel Smith 1992 -
.... 10 [86] Cynthia Diane Beery 1958 -
.... +[87] Karl Warren Bauder 1954 -
.... 11 [88] Aaron Thomas Bauder 1988 -
.... +[89] Julie Goetz 1989 -
.... 12 [90] Zoey Grace Bauder 2013 -
.... 11 [91] Joshua Ryan Bauder 1985 -
.... 12 [18] Lila Kay Bauder 2008 -
.... +[92] Bethany Kay Leonard 1987 -
.... 12 [18] Lila Kay Bauder 2008 -
.... *2nd Wife of [91] Joshua Ryan Bauder:
.... +[93] Tiffanie Burtnett (Rau) 1981 -

.... 12 [94] Cheyenne Rau 2006 -
.... 12 [95] Samantha Rau 2007 -
.... 10 [96] Cheryl Denise Beery 1963 -
.... +[97] Larry Philip Shell Jr. 1962 -
.... 11 [98] Lauren Ashley Shell 1987 -
.... 11 [99] Jillian Leigh Shell 1989 -
.... +[100] Luis Carlos Agramont 1985 -
.... 12 [101] Leighton Agramont 2014 -
.... *2nd Husband of [96] Cheryl Denise Beery:
.... +[102] Dick Aldes Holihan Jr. 1956 -
.... 9 [103] Carol Jean Durbin 1940 -
.... +[104] Arthur Bidner 1932 -
.... 10 [105] Susan Jeanette Bidner 1963 -
.... +[106] James Edward Burns 1964 -
.... 11 [107] Benjamin Alexander Burns 2002 -
.... 8 [140] Berniece Naomi Barkley 1902 - 1989
.... +[141] Bruce Adams
.... 8 [142] Nellie Barkley 1900 - 1948
.... +[19] Ufa Henry Durbin 1899 - 1958
.... 9 [20] Marvin Darrell Durbin 1924 - 1992
.... +[21] Susan Mae Webster 1946 -
.... 10 [22] Victoria Lynn Durbin 1966 -
.... 10 [23] Tamara Sue Durbin 1974 -
.... *2nd Wife of [20] Marvin Darrell Durbin:
.... +[24] Joan LaDuke
.... 10 [25] Donna Rae LaDuke 1957 -
.... 10 [26] Richard Lee LaDuke 1960 -
.... *3rd Wife of [20] Marvin Darrell Durbin:
.... +[27] Betty Lee Schmidt
.... 10 [28] Darrell Lee Durbin 1948 -
.... 10 [29] Carolyn Sue Durbin 1949 - 1957
.... 10 [30] David Lawrence Durbin - 1996
.... 9 [31] Jack Calvin Durbin 1925 - 2012
.... +[32] Mae Dean Wooley 1928 - 2010
.... 10 [33] Dorothy Annette Durbin 1955 - 1955
.... 10 [34] Debra Jeanette Durbin 1955 -
.... 10 [35] Blake Calvin Durbin 1967 -
.... 9 [36] Leonard Leroy Durbin 1927 - 1995
.... 9 [37] Betty Jewell Durbin 1931 -
.... +[38] Winfred Lee Carson, Sr. 1920 - 1991
.... 10 [39] Winfred Lee Carson, Jr. 1954 -
.... +[40] Sanda Kandi 1946 -
.... 11 [41] Terrance Dale Carson 1979 -
.... +[42] Dionne Petersen
.... 12 [43] Tyler Dale Carson 1999 -
.... 12 [44] Taylor Nichole Carson 2002 -
.... 12 [45] Tiffanie Jean Carson 2002 -
.... 11 [46] Jason Lee Carson 1981 -
.... 11 [47] Nicole Neela Carson 1988 -
.... 10 [48] Bonnie Lee Carson 1957 -

.... +[49] Robert William Johnson
.... *2nd Husband of [48] Bonnie Lee Carson:
.... +[50] Kevin Lee Peck
.... *3rd Husband of [48] Bonnie Lee Carson:
.... +[51] Daniel Miller
.... 11 [52] Daniel Lee Miller 2000 -
.... 9 [53] Doris May Durbin 1932 - 2014
.... +[54] Ovid Maurice Wooley 1933 - 2004
.... 10 [55] Martha Ann Wooley 1953 -
.... +[56] Paul John Barthelome Volcherick
.... 11 [57] Lane Edward Volcherick 1980 -
.... 10 [58] Ovid Maurice Wooley, Jr. 1955 -
.... 10 [59] Richard Lynn Wooley 1959 -
.... +[60] Brenda Kay Miller 1961 -
.... 11 [61] Jason Neil Wooley 1976 -
.... 11 [62] Kaveh Marlin Wooley 1978 -
.... 11 [63] Kapril Michelle Wooley 1987 -
.... *2nd Wife of [59] Richard Lynn Wooley:
.... +[64] Rhonda Robberson
.... 11 [65] Larry Robberson 1977 -
.... 10 [66] Beverly Sue Wooley 1962 -
.... 10 [67] Peggy Jean Wooley 1964 -
.... +[68] Ricky Dean Shawback
.... 11 [69] Peggy LeeAnn Shawback 1984 -
.... 11 [70] Chrystal May Shawback 1986 -
.... 11 [71] Lauane Marrie Shawback 1988 -
.... 9 [72] Peggy Joyce Durbin 1936 -
.... +[73] Irvin Lee Beery 1934 - 2012
.... 10 [74] Vicki Lynn Beery 1956 -
.... +[75] Jerry Allan Smith 1954 -
.... 11 [76] Andrew Philip Smith 1985 -
.... 11 [77] Anna Elizabeth Smith 1987 -
.... +[78] Noah Daniel McLaughlin 1984 -
.... 12 [79] Harley Lyne McLaughlin 2009 -
.... 12 [80] Tristin Robert Lee McLaughlin 2011 - 2011
.... 12 [81] Rustin Rae McLaughlin 2011 -
.... 12 [82] Hope Elizabeth McLaughlin 2012 -
.... 11 [83] Lydia Abigail Smith 1991 -
.... +[84] Aaron Cress 1991 -
.... 11 [85] Leah Rachel Smith 1992 -
.... 10 [86] Cynthia Diane Beery 1958 -
.... +[87] Karl Warren Bauder 1954 -
.... 11 [88] Aaron Thomas Bauder 1988 -
.... +[89] Julie Goetz 1989 -
.... 12 [90] Zoey Grace Bauder 2013 -
.... 11 [91] Joshua Ryan Bauder 1985 -
.... 12 [18] Lila Kay Bauder 2008 -
.... +[92] Bethany Kay Leonard 1987 -
.... 12 [18] Lila Kay Bauder 2008 -

.... *2nd Wife of [91] Joshua Ryan Bauder:
.... +[93] Tiffanie Burtnett (Rau) 1981 -
.... 12 [94] Cheyenne Rau 2006 -
.... 12 [95] Samantha Rau 2007 -
.... 10 [96] Cheryl Denise Beery 1963 -
.... +[97] Larry Philip Shell Jr. 1962 -
.... 11 [98] Lauren Ashley Shell 1987 -
.... 11 [99] Jillian Leigh Shell 1989 -
.... +[100] Luis Carlos Agramont 1985 -
.... 12 [101] Leighton Agramont 2014 -
.... *2nd Husband of [96] Cheryl Denise Beery:
.... +[102] Dick Aldes Holihan Jr. 1956 -
.... 9 [103] Carol Jean Durbin 1940 -
.... +[104] Arthur Bidner 1932 -
.... 10 [105] Susan Jeanette Bidner 1963 -
.... +[106] James Edward Burns 1964 -
.... 11 [107] Benjamin Alexander Burns 2002 -
.... 5 Henry Barkley 1797 - 1859
.... +Sarah (Sally) Brown - 1849
.... 6 Maria J. Barkley
.... 6 Elizabeth R. Barkley
.... 6 John L. Barkley 1840 - 1894
.... 6 William S. Barkley
.... 6 George H. B. Barkley
.... 6 Margaret George Ann Barkley
.... 6 David William Barkley 1832 - 1834
.... 5 John Barkley 1801 - 1838
.... +Margaret P. Buchanan 1804 - 1881
.... 5 Joseph Barkley 1812 - 1879
.... +Florence/Florella C. Wood 1811 - 1871
.... 6 Barkley Barkley
.... 6 Elizabeth S. Barkley
.... 6 James H. Barkley
.... 6 Joseph Henry Louis Barkley
.... +[109] Mary Elizabeth Barber 1862 - 1930
.... 7 [110] Rena B. Barkley 1882 - 1935
.... 7 [111] Stella Mae Barkley 1884 - 1971
.... +[112] Orris Estes
.... *2nd Husband of [111] Stella Mae Barkley:
.... +[113] Cal Chastain
.... 8 [114] Calvin Chastain, Jr.
.... 7 [115] Oren Perry Barkley 1886 - 1959
.... 7 [116] Josephine Edna Barkley 1888 - 1932
.... +[117] Joe Minarick
.... 7 [118] Arthur Harrison Barkley 1889 - 1974
.... +[119] Mary Aletha Steele
.... 8 [120] Harry Arthur Barkley
.... +[121] Margaret Douglas
.... 9 [122] Steve Barkley
.... 9 [14] Robert Louis Barkley

.... +[15] Anna May
.... 10 [16] Kenny Barkley
.... 10 [17] Bradley Barkley
.... 8 [14] Robert Louis Barkley
.... +[15] Anna May
.... 9 [16] Kenny Barkley
.... 9 [17] Bradley Barkley
.... 7 [123] Elizabeth Jay Barkley 1893 - 1975
.... +[124] Harry Beaufort
.... 8 [125] Harry Beaufort, Jr.
.... 8 [126] Dorothy Beaufort 1920 -
.... +[127] Spivey
.... 9 [128] Keith Douglas Spivey 1948 -
.... 9 [129] Glynn Lyneau Spivey 1951 -
.... *2nd Husband of [126] Dorothy Beaufort:
.... +[130] Kelly
.... 8 [131] Robert Lewis Beaufort
.... +[132] Fairy - 1977
.... 9 [133] Galen Beaufort
.... 9 [134] Becky Beaufort
.... 7 [135] Alma Myrtle Barkley 1895 - 1988
.... +[136] Arthur Kirkner 1881 - 1921
.... 7 [137] Marion Harvey Barkley 1898 -
.... +[138] Ruby Moberly
.... 7 [139] Nellie Barkley 1900 - 1948
.... +[19] Ufa Henry Durbin 1899 - 1958
.... 8 [20] Marvin Darrell Durbin 1924 - 1992
.... +[21] Susan Mae Webster 1946 -
.... 9 [22] Victoria Lynn Durbin 1966 -
.... 9 [23] Tamara Sue Durbin 1974 -
.... *2nd Wife of [20] Marvin Darrell Durbin:
.... +[24] Joan LaDuke
.... 9 [25] Donna Rae LaDuke 1957 -
.... 9 [26] Richard Lee LaDuke 1960 -
.... *3rd Wife of [20] Marvin Darrell Durbin:
.... +[27] Betty Lee Schmidt
.... 9 [28] Darrell Lee Durbin 1948 -
.... 9 [29] Carolyn Sue Durbin 1949 - 1957
.... 9 [30] David Lawrence Durbin - 1996
.... 8 [31] Jack Calvin Durbin 1925 - 2012
.... +[32] Mae Dean Wooley 1928 - 2010
.... 9 [33] Dorothy Annette Durbin 1955 - 1955
.... 9 [34] Debra Jeanette Durbin 1955 -
.... 9 [35] Blake Calvin Durbin 1967 -
.... 8 [36] Leonard Leroy Durbin 1927 - 1995
.... 8 [37] Betty Jewell Durbin 1931 -
.... +[38] Winfred Lee Carson, Sr. 1920 - 1991
.... 9 [39] Winfred Lee Carson, Jr. 1954 -
.... +[40] Sanda Kandi 1946 -
.... 10 [41] Terrance Dale Carson 1979 -

+[42] Dionne Petersen
11 [43] Tyler Dale Carson 1999 -
11 [44] Taylor Nichole Carson 2002 -
11 [45] Tiffanie Jean Carson 2002 -
10 [46] Jason Lee Carson 1981 -
10 [47] Nicole Neela Carson 1988 -
9 [48] Bonnie Lee Carson 1957 -
+[49] Robert William Johnson
*2nd Husband of [48] Bonnie Lee Carson:
+[50] Kevin Lee Peck
*3rd Husband of [48] Bonnie Lee Carson:
+[51] Daniel Miller
10 [52] Daniel Lee Miller 2000 -
8 [53] Doris May Durbin 1932 - 2014
+[54] Ovid Maurice Wooley 1933 - 2004
9 [55] Martha Ann Wooley 1953 -
+[56] Paul John Barthelome Volcherick
10 [57] Lane Edward Volcherick 1980 -
9 [58] Ovid Maurice Wooley, Jr. 1955 -
9 [59] Richard Lynn Wooley 1959 -
+[60] Brenda Kay Miller 1961 -
10 [61] Jason Neil Wooley 1976 -
10 [62] Kaveh Marlin Wooley 1978 -
10 [63] Kapril Michelle Wooley 1987 -
*2nd Wife of [59] Richard Lynn Wooley:
+[64] Rhonda Robberson
10 [65] Larry Robberson 1977 -
9 [66] Beverly Sue Wooley 1962 -
9 [67] Peggy Jean Wooley 1964 -
+[68] Ricky Dean Shawback
10 [69] Peggy LeeAnn Shawback 1984 -
10 [70] Chrystal May Shawback 1986 -
10 [71] Lauane Marrie Shawback 1988 -
8 [72] Peggy Joyce Durbin 1936 -
+[73] Irvin Lee Beery 1934 - 2012
9 [74] Vicki Lynn Beery 1956 -
+[75] Jerry Allan Smith 1954 -
10 [76] Andrew Philip Smith 1985 -
10 [77] Anna Elizabeth Smith 1987 -
+[78] Noah Daniel McLaughlin 1984 -
11 [79] Harley Lyne McLaughlin 2009 -
11 [80] Tristin Robert Lee McLaughlin 2011 - 2011
11 [81] Rustin Rae McLaughlin 2011 -
11 [82] Hope Elizabeth McLaughlin 2012 -
10 [83] Lydia Abigail Smith 1991 -
+[84] Aaron Cress 1991 -
10 [85] Leah Rachel Smith 1992 -
9 [86] Cynthia Diane Beery 1958 -
+[87] Karl Warren Bauder 1954 -

.... 10 [88] Aaron Thomas Bauder 1988 -
.... +[89] Julie Goetz 1989 -
.... 11 [90] Zoey Grace Bauder 2013 -
.... 10 [91] Joshua Ryan Bauder 1985 -
.... 11 [18] Lila Kay Bauder 2008 -
.... +[92] Bethany Kay Leonard 1987 -
.... 11 [18] Lila Kay Bauder 2008 -
.... *2nd Wife of [91] Joshua Ryan Bauder:
.... +[93] Tiffanie Burtnett (Rau) 1981 -
.... 11 [94] Cheyenne Rau 2006 -
.... 11 [95] Samantha Rau 2007 -
.... 9 [96] Cheryl Denise Beery 1963 -
.... +[97] Larry Philip Shell Jr. 1962 -
.... 10 [98] Lauren Ashley Shell 1987 -
.... 10 [99] Jillian Leigh Shell 1989 -
.... +[100] Luis Carlos Agramont 1985 -
.... 11 [101] Leighton Agramont 2014 -
.... *2nd Husband of [96] Cheryl Denise Beery:
.... +[102] Dick Aldes Holihan Jr. 1956 -
.... 8 [103] Carol Jean Durbin 1940 -
.... +[104] Arthur Bidner 1932 -
.... 9 [105] Susan Jeanette Bidner 1963 -
.... +[106] James Edward Burns 1964 -
.... 10 [107] Benjamin Alexander Burns 2002 -
.... 7 [140] Berniece Naomi Barkley 1902 - 1989
.... +[141] Bruce Adams
.... 7 [142] Nellie Barkley 1900 - 1948
.... +[19] Ufa Henry Durbin 1899 - 1958
.... 8 [20] Marvin Darrell Durbin 1924 - 1992
.... +[21] Susan Mae Webster 1946 -
.... 9 [22] Victoria Lynn Durbin 1966 -
.... 9 [23] Tamara Sue Durbin 1974 -
.... *2nd Wife of [20] Marvin Darrell Durbin:
.... +[24] Joan LaDuke
.... 9 [25] Donna Rae LaDuke 1957 -
.... 9 [26] Richard Lee LaDuke 1960 -
.... *3rd Wife of [20] Marvin Darrell Durbin:
.... +[27] Betty Lee Schmidt
.... 9 [28] Darrell Lee Durbin 1948 -
.... 9 [29] Carolyn Sue Durbin 1949 - 1957
.... 9 [30] David Lawrence Durbin - 1996
.... 8 [31] Jack Calvin Durbin 1925 - 2012
.... +[32] Mae Dean Wooley 1928 - 2010
.... 9 [33] Dorothy Annette Durbin 1955 - 1955
.... 9 [34] Debra Jeanette Durbin 1955 -
.... 9 [35] Blake Calvin Durbin 1967 -
.... 8 [36] Leonard Leroy Durbin 1927 - 1995
.... 8 [37] Betty Jewell Durbin 1931 -
.... +[38] Winfred Lee Carson, Sr. 1920 - 1991
.... 9 [39] Winfred Lee Carson, Jr. 1954 -

.... +[40] Sanda Kandi 1946 -
.... 10 [41] Terrance Dale Carson 1979 -
.... +[42] Dionne Petersen
.... 11 [43] Tyler Dale Carson 1999 -
.... 11 [44] Taylor Nichole Carson 2002 -
.... 11 [45] Tiffanie Jean Carson 2002 -
.... 10 [46] Jason Lee Carson 1981 -
.... 10 [47] Nicole Neela Carson 1988 -
.... 9 [48] Bonnie Lee Carson 1957 -
.... +[49] Robert William Johnson
.... *2nd Husband of [48] Bonnie Lee Carson:
.... +[50] Kevin Lee Peck
.... *3rd Husband of [48] Bonnie Lee Carson:
.... +[51] Daniel Miller
.... 10 [52] Daniel Lee Miller 2000 -
.... 8 [53] Doris May Durbin 1932 - 2014
.... +[54] Ovid Maurice Wooley 1933 - 2004
.... 9 [55] Martha Ann Wooley 1953 -
.... +[56] Paul John Barthelome Volcherick
.... 10 [57] Lane Edward Volcherick 1980 -
.... 9 [58] Ovid Maurice Wooley, Jr. 1955 -
.... 9 [59] Richard Lynn Wooley 1959 -
.... +[60] Brenda Kay Miller 1961 -
.... 10 [61] Jason Neil Wooley 1976 -
.... 10 [62] Kaveh Marlin Wooley 1978 -
.... 10 [63] Kapril Michelle Wooley 1987 -
.... *2nd Wife of [59] Richard Lynn Wooley:
.... +[64] Rhonda Robberson
.... 10 [65] Larry Robberson 1977 -
.... 9 [66] Beverly Sue Wooley 1962 -
.... 9 [67] Peggy Jean Wooley 1964 -
.... +[68] Ricky Dean Shawback
.... 10 [69] Peggy LeeAnn Shawback 1984 -
.... 10 [70] Chrystal May Shawback 1986 -
.... 10 [71] Lauane Marrie Shawback 1988 -
.... 8 [72] Peggy Joyce Durbin 1936 -
.... +[73] Irvin Lee Beery 1934 - 2012
.... 9 [74] Vicki Lynn Beery 1956 -
.... +[75] Jerry Allan Smith 1954 -
.... 10 [76] Andrew Philip Smith 1985 -
.... 10 [77] Anna Elizabeth Smith 1987 -
.... +[78] Noah Daniel McLaughlin 1984 -
.... 11 [79] Harley Lyne McLaughlin 2009 -
.... 11 [80] Tristin Robert Lee McLaughlin 2011 - 2011
.... 11 [81] Rustin Rae McLaughlin 2011 -
.... 11 [82] Hope Elizabeth McLaughlin 2012 -
.... 10 [83] Lydia Abigail Smith 1991 -
.... +[84] Aaron Cress 1991 -
.... 10 [85] Leah Rachel Smith 1992 -

.... 9 [86] Cynthia Diane Beery 1958 -
.... +[87] Karl Warren Bauder 1954 -
.... 10 [88] Aaron Thomas Bauder 1988 -
.... +[89] Julie Goetz 1989 -
.... 11 [90] Zoey Grace Bauder 2013 -
.... 10 [91] Joshua Ryan Bauder 1985 -
.... 11 [18] Lila Kay Bauder 2008 -
.... +[92] Bethany Kay Leonard 1987 -
.... 11 [18] Lila Kay Bauder 2008 -
.... *2nd Wife of [91] Joshua Ryan Bauder:
.... +[93] Tiffanie Burtnett (Rau) 1981 -
.... 11 [94] Cheyenne Rau 2006 -
.... 11 [95] Samantha Rau 2007 -
.... 9 [96] Cheryl Denise Beery 1963 -
.... +[97] Larry Philip Shell Jr. 1962 -
.... 10 [98] Lauren Ashley Shell 1987 -
.... 10 [99] Jillian Leigh Shell 1989 -
.... +[100] Luis Carlos Agramont 1985 -
.... 11 [101] Leighton Agramont 2014 -
.... *2nd Husband of [96] Cheryl Denise Beery:
.... +[102] Dick Aldes Holihan Jr. 1956 -
.... 8 [103] Carol Jean Durbin 1940 -
.... +[104] Arthur Bidner 1932 -
.... 9 [105] Susan Jeanette Bidner 1963 -
.... +[106] James Edward Burns 1964 -
.... 10 [107] Benjamin Alexander Burns 2002 -
.... 6 Laura Florilla Barkley
.... 6 Rebecca Barkley
.... 6 Mary Jane Barkley 1835 -
.... +Andrew Henry Hanna 1813 -
.... 7 Ellison Hanna 1845 -
.... 7 Thomas Hanna 1850 -
.... 7 Charles Hanna 1853 -
.... 7 Alice Hanna 1857 -
.... 7 Mary J. Hanna 1860 -
.... 6 William G. Barkley 1838 -
.... 6 Margaret Salina Barkley 1840 -
.... 6 Lucy Maxwell Barkley 1841 - 1908
.... +Peter Carmerer Smith 1837 - 1915
.... 7 Sadie Smith 1878 -
.... +William A. Wedding
.... 7 Laura A. Smith 1880 -
.... +G. E. Denniston
.... 7 Jessie L. Smith 1884 -
.... +Eugene Denniston
.... 6 Louisa A. Barkley 1842 -
.... 6 John C. Barkley
.... 5 Katherine Barkley 1808 - 1866
.... +John P. McKinney
.... 5 Mary B. "Polly" Barkley 1824 - 1903

.... +John H. Wood 1823 -
.... 6   Florilla Wood 1840 -
.... 6   Joseph H. Wood 1842 -
.... 4   Henry Barkley 1779 -
.... 4   Katherine Barkley
.... 4   Mary B. Barkley
..... 2   Lucy Barclay
..... 2   Robert Barclay 1648 - 1690

Index of Individuals

61

BARLEY
PICTURE GALLERY

JOSEPH B. BARKLEY
1851 — 1923

PERRY H. BARKLEY
1824 — 1885

BARKLEY

JOSEPH B.
1851 1923

JULIA E.
1872
MAY 20 1956

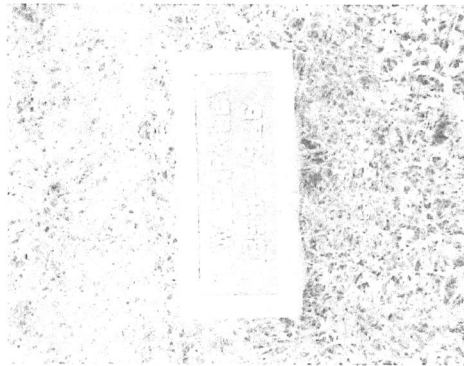

Mount Zion Cemetery, New Richmond, Clermont County, Ohio

No grave found for Asa Tell Barkley, born March 1856, Clermont County, Ohio, married Elizabeth Fritz, lived in Franklin Co, Kansas, 1920

Old and New Calvary Cemetery
St. Rt. 756, Washington Township
GPS N38° 52.170 W084° 10.202, Elev. 780, within 21 ft.

Take St. Rt. 52 from Cincinnati, pass through New Richmond. At Point Pleasant make a left on St. Rt. 232, make a right onto St. Rt. 756. Pass Washington Township Park. Cross St. Rt. 743. Old Cemetery located on right across from church and New Calvary Cemetery located by the church. Park at church. Easy Access.

Barber, Eliza Jane

Barber, Margaret

Barber, Mattie A.B.

Barker, Sue Moreton

Barkley, Bell R.

Barkley, Florella

Barkley, George

Barkley, John

Barkley, Joseph H.

Old and New Calvary Cemetery
St. Rt. 756, Washington Township
GPS N38° 52.170 W084° 10.202, Elev. 780, within 21 ft.

Take St. Rt. 52 from Cincinnati, pass through New Richmond. At Point Pleasant make a left on St. Rt. 232, make a right onto St. Rt. 756. Pass Washington Township Park. Cross St. Rt. 743. Old Cemetery located on right across from church and New Calvary Cemetery located by the church. Park at church. Easy Access.

Barkley, Joseph

Barkley, Lizzie S.

Barkley, Margaret

Barkley, Rebecca

Barkley, Sarah R.

Barkley, W. G.

Barkley, William stone

Barkley, William

Old and New Calvary Cemetery

St. Rt. 756, Washington Township
GPS N38° 52.170 W084° 10.202, Elev. 780, within 21 ft.

Take St. Rt. 52 from Cincinnati, pass through New Richmond. At Point Pleasant make a left on St. Rt. 232, make a right onto St. Rt. 756. Pass Washington Township Park. Cross St. Rt. 743. Old Cemetery located on right across from church and New Calvary Cemetery located by the church. Park at church. Easy Access.

Manning, Augusta

Manning, Charity stone

Manning, Charity

Manning, George G.

Manning, Gerald R.

Manning, Josephine Irwin

Manning, Marsail

Manning, Mary Helen

Manning, Mary

Old and New Calvary Cemetery

St. Rt. 756, Washington Township
GPS N38° 52.170 W084° 10.202, Elev. 780, within 21 ft.

Take St. Rt. 52 from Cincinnati, pass through New Richmond. At Point Pleasant make a left on St. Rt. 232, make a right onto St. Rt. 756. Pass Washington Township Park. Cross St. Rt. 743. Old Cemetery located on right across from church and New Calvary Cemetery located by the church. Park at church. Easy Access.

Manning, Nathan single grave

Manning, Nathan

Manning, Oscar J.

Manning, Rachel

Manning, Squire and Rachel, Mother and Father Inscript

Manning, Squire

Manning, William S.

OLD CALVARY CEMETERY
East of Felicity on State Road 756 in Washington Twp, Clermont Co, Ohio

William Barkley & Rebecca Barkley
b. 17 Nov. 1822   d. 21 Mar. 1904

§ Certificate
No. 2200

The United States of America.

To all to whom these presents shall come, Greeting:

Whereas, Joseph Barkley of Clermont County Ohio

has deposited in the General Land Office of the United States, a certificate of the Register of the Land Office at Palestine whereby it appears that full payment has been made by the said Joseph Barkley according to the provisions of the act of Congress of the 24th of April, 1820, entitled "An act making further provision for the sale of the Public Lands," for The North West fraction (East) of the South West (pic) of Section Nays, in Township North of Range Eleven West, in the District of lands subject to sale, at Palestine, Illinois containing four hundred and fifty Acres and Seventy three hundredths of an Acre according to the official plat of the survey of the said Lands, returned to the General Land Office by the Surveyor General, which said tract has been purchased by the said Joseph Barkley

NOW KNOW YE, That the **UNITED STATES OF AMERICA,** in consideration of the premises, and in conformity with the several acts of Congress, in such case made and provided, have given and granted, and, by these presents, do give and grant, unto the said Joseph Barkley and to his heirs, the said tract above described: To Have and to Hold the same, together with all the rights, privileges, immunities and appurtenances, of whatsoever nature thereunto belonging, unto the said Joseph Barkley and to his heirs and assigns forever.

In testimony whereof, I, Andrew Jackson, **PRESIDENT OF THE UNITED STATES OF AMERICA,** have caused these Letters to be made Patent, and the Seal of the General Land Office to be hereunto affixed.

Given under my hand, at the City of Washington, the sixth day of June in the year of our Lord, one thousand eight hundred and thirty one, and of the Independence of the United States the fifty fifth

By the President,

A. J.

Commissioner of the General Land Office.

73

Back Row: Mary Elizabeth Barber Barkley, Joseph Henry Louis Barkley, Rena B. Barkley

Front: Stella Mae Barkley and Josephine Edna Barkley

MISSOURI STATE BOARD OF HEALTH
BUREAU OF VITAL STATISTICS
CERTIFICATE OF DEATH

1 PLACE OF DEATH

County _Cass_

Township _Austin_
or

Village ....

or

City _Archie_ (NO. , St.; Ward)

Registration District No. _147_

Primary Registration District No. _408_

File No. **22222**

Registered No. _14_

(If death occurred in a hospital or institution, give its NAME instead of street and number.)

2 FULL NAME _Mary E. Barkley_

PERSONAL AND STATISTICAL PARTICULARS	MEDICAL CERTIFICATE OF DEATH
3 SEX _F_ **4 COLOR OR RACE** _White_ **5 SINGLE MARRIED WIDOWED OR DIVORCED** (Write the word) _Married_	**16 DATE OF DEATH** _July 1st 1930_ (Month) (Day) (Year)
6 DATE OF BIRTH _April 1st 1862_ (Month) (Day) (Year)	**17** I HEREBY CERTIFY, that I attended deceased from _June 30_ 1930 to _July 1st_ 1930, that I last saw her alive on _July 1st_ 1930, and that death occurred, on the date stated above, at _1-30_ a. m.
7 AGE _68_ yrs. _2_ mos. _0_ ds. **If LESS than 1 day;....hrs. or....min.?**	The CAUSE OF DEATH* was as follows: _Creeping Paralysis_
8 OCCUPATION (a) Trade, profession, or particular kind of work _Housewife_ (b) General nature of industry, business, or establishment in which employed (or employer)	_73 A 4 mos. 2 ds._ (Duration)
9 BIRTHPLACE (City or town, State or foreign country) _Ill._	**CONTRIBUTORY** (Secondary) (Duration) yrs. mos. ds.
PARENTS **10 NAME OF FATHER** _J. K. Barker_	(Signed) _B. B. Tout_ M.D.
11 BIRTHPLACE OF FATHER (City or town, State or foreign country) _Don't know_	_7/1st_ 1930 (Address) _Archie Mo._
12 MAIDEN NAME OF MOTHER _Manning_	*State the Disease Causing Death, or in deaths from Violent Causes, state (1) Means of Injury; and (2) whether Accidental, Suicidal or Homicidal.
13 BIRTHPLACE OF MOTHER (City or town, State or foreign country) _Ill._	**18 LENGTH OF RESIDENCE** (For Hospitals, Institutions, Transients, or Recent Residents) At place of death ....yrs....mos....ds. In the State ....yrs....mos....ds.
14 THE ABOVE IS TRUE TO THE BEST OF MY KNOWLEDGE (Informant) _Mrs. Stella Estes_ (Address) _Independence Mo._	Where was disease contracted if not at place of death? Former or usual residence
15 Filed _7/1_ 1930 _Dr. B. B. Tout_ Registrar	**19 PLACE OF BURIAL OR REMOVAL** _Mt. Olivet Adrian_ **DATE OF BURIAL** _July 2, 1930_ **20 UNDERTAKER** _Creath & Son_ **ADDRESS** _Adrian Mo._

Great Grandmother Mary Elizabeth Barber

mother of Mary Barber who married Joseph Henry Louis Barkley

Elizabeth Barkley Beaufort Arthur Barkley, Alma Barkley Kirkner

Great Grandma Mary Elizabeth Barber

Nellie Barkley Durbin with brother Oren Perry Barkley

Arthur Barkley and Family

Stella Chastain, Alma Kirkner, Calvin Chastain, Elizabeth Beaufort

Left: Arthur and Margaret Barkley
Right: Robert Louis Barkley
Bottom Right: Harry Arthur Barkley (son)
   Arthur and Margaret
   Robert Louis Barkley (son)

Alma Barkley and husband Arthur Kirkner

Marion Barkley and wife Ruby Moberly

Top: Bernice Naomi Barkley Adams, Stella May Barkley Kirkner,
Nellie Barkley Durbin, Alma Barkley Kirkner, Sisters

Left: Nellie Barkley; Right: Nellie Barkley

Middle: Joseph Henry Louis Barkley, daughter Nellie Barkley

Bernice and Nellie Barkley, ca 1910--Nellie Barkley

Bernice Naomi Barkley and Bruce Adams

MARRIAGE LICENSE

STATE OF MISSOURI, }ss.
COUNTY OF _Bates_

This License authorizes any Judge of a Court of Record or any Justice of the Peace, or any licensed or ordained Preacher of the Gospel, who is a Citizen of the United States, or who is a resident of and a Pastor of any Church in this State to solemnize Marriage between _Ufa Henry Durbin_ of _Adrian_ in the County of _Bates_ and State of _Mo_ who is over the age of twenty-one years, and _Nellie Barkley_ of _Kansas City_ in the County of _Jackson_ and State of _Mo_ who is over the age of eighteen years,

WITNESS MY HAND, as Recorder of Deeds with the Seal of Office hereto affixed at my Office in _Butler Mo_ this _29_ day of _June_ 192_3_

By _Christine Curtainger_ (seal) _Chas H Arguenright_
Deputy _Recorder of Deeds_

STATE OF MISSOURI, }ss.
COUNTY OF _Bates_

This is to Certify, That the undersigned, _minister of the Gospel_ did, at his _personal home_ in said County, on the _30_ day of _June_ A. D. 192_3_ unite in Marriage the above named persons, and I further certify that I am legally qualified under the Laws of the State of Missouri to solemnize Marriages.

W. B. Muir

The foregoing Certificate of Marriage was filed for Record in my office on the ___ day of _July_ A. D. 1923

By _Christine Curtainger_ _Chas H Arguenright_
Deputy _Recorder of Deeds_

Nellie Barkley Durbin and Ufa Henry Durbin

Son Marvin Darrell Durbin

Marvin Durbin

Top Left to Right: Betty Lee, son Darrell, Marvin Darrell Durbin; Middle & Right: Marvin

Bottom Left to Right: Darrell and Katherine (12/1980), Son Christopher and Family

Top, Left to Right: Jack & Mae Dean Wedding, Jack, Jack holding Debbie
Middle, Left to Right: Mae Dean holding Debbie, Jack holding Debbie, Debbie's Wedding Picture
Bottom: Family Group Picture: Spruce Street, Wichita, Kansas

Leonard Leroy Durbin

(Leonard never married)

Betty Jewell Durbin Carson

Top, Left to Right: Wedding Photo and Portrait in Woods
Middle, Left: Winfred (Kit) Lee Carson, Bonnie Lee Carson, Nicole Carson
Left to Right: Jason Lee Carson, Sandra K. Carson, Winfred L. Carson
        Nicole Carson, Terry Carson, Betty J. Carson
        Tiffanie Carson, Taylor Carson, Tyler Carson
Right Bottom: Betty, Granddaughter Nicole,
Grandson Daniel Miller, Daughter Bonnie Miller   92

Top, Left to Right: Carol and Art Bidner Wedding Picture
    Art & Peggy with Susan
Middle, Left Jim Burns, Susan Bidner Burns, Carol Jean Durbin Bidner
Right: Carol Jean Bidner, Susan Bidner Burns, Peggy Durbin Beery
Bottom: Carol Jean Durbin, age 3

Left to Right: Betty Jewell Durbin Carson, Doris May Durbin Wooley,
Peggy Joyce Durbin Beery, Carol Jean Durbin Bidner
At Parents' Graves in Oak Hill Cemetery, Butler, MO

Brother Leonard Leroy Durbin Grave, Oak Hill Cemetery next to parents

Durbin Family Reunion
August 24, 1992
Maize, Kansas

Left to Right: Marvin Darrell Durbin, Jack Calvin Durbin, Leonard Leroy Durbin,
Betty Jewell Durbin Carson, Doris May Durbin Wooley,
Peggy Joyce Durbin Beery, Carol Jean Durbin Bidner

Top: Doris and Maurice Wooley
Middle: Doris May Durbin Wooley
Bottom: Doris May Durbin & Betty Jewell Durbin
ca: 1936

November 21, 2003

Mr. and Mrs. Winfred Carson
366 Sease Hill Rd.
Lexington, SC 29072

Dear Mr. and Mrs. Carson,

I would like to express my deepest gratitude for the contributions of your son during his time with HMM-264. From the onset of the deployment I knew the squadron would encounter many unforeseen challenges as the nation entered armed conflict in the Middle East. With the flexibility of a Marine Expeditionary Unit, our role was unknown at first but as time unfolded our capabilities were used to the fullest.

The success of the "Black Knights" would not have been possible without the exceptional efforts of Terry in the Airframes Division. Frequently working long hours in a demanding environment, he ensured the readiness of the CH-46E Phrogs for any assigned mission. As it turned out, the squadron conducted the full spectrum of military operations, from combat operations in Northern Iraq to a presence mission off the coast of Eastern Africa, and ending with a humanitarian mission in support of the Liberian crisis.

It is the hard work, total dedication, and commitment of Terry that maintains the legacy of the Marine Corps. I would like to personally thank you for your continued support of his service to this great nation and his fellow Marines. I am very proud of his meritorious promotion to the rank of Sergeant and I am looking forward to his future contributions to this squadron. As his parents, you can be proud of his many accomplishments.

Sincerely,

N. John Torres
Commanding Officer

Red Bank Marine heads back to serve in Iraq

U.S. Marine Staff Sgt. Terrance Dale Carson, who grew up in Lexington, has returned to Iraq this month.

Terry and his wife Dionne have three children, Tyler 5, Taylor 3 and Tiffany 2. They make their home in Red Bank. He is the son of Sandra and Winfred Carson Jr. of Lexington, and grandson of Betty J. Carson of the VA Office.

Terry served a tour of combat duty in northern Iraq, a mission off the coast of eastern Africa, and a humanitarian mission in the Liberian crisis for which Carson received a letter of commendation. "The success of the Black Knights would not have been possible without the exceptional efforts of Terry in the Airframes Division frequently working long hours in a demanding environment," wrote Lt. Col. John Torres, Commanding Officer in a letter to his parents in December, 2004.

Staff Sgt. Terry Carson

The mission of the Marine Medium Helicopter Squadron is to provide assault support for combat troops, supplies and equipment during amphibious operations and subsequent operations ashore. The HMM squadron, operating medium vertical lift assault aircraft (CH-46E Sea Knights), is organized to conduct operations as an entire squadron. Routinely, HMM squadrons provide the foundation for an aviation combat element (ACE) of any level Marine Air-Ground Task Force (MAGTF) mission that may include conventional assault support tasks and special operations.

HMM-264 is a CH-46E squadron which performs the Assault Support function for the Marine Air-Ground Task Force (MAGTF). Assault support is the use of aircraft to provide tactical mobility and logistic support, movement of high priority cargo and personnel. Assault support missions are: Combat Assault Transport, Air Delivery, Air Evacuation, Air Logistical Support, Battlespace Illumination, and Tactical Recovery of Aircraft and Personnel (TRAP). These missions provide the MAGTF Commander with mobility required to mass and sustain his combat power at decisive places and times. The squadron can be employed as a subordinate unit to the Marine Air Group, or can serve as the Air Combat Element (ACE) of a Marine Expeditionary Unit (MEU). The MEU ACE is a Marine Medium Helicopter squadron augmented with additional types of aircraft to form a composite squadron. These detachments include equipment and personnel to support CH-53E Super Stallions, UH-1N Hueys, and AH-1W Super Cobras. ACE assets may also include fixed-wing aircraft such as the AV-8B Harrier and/or KC-130 Hercules squadrons. The ACE is capable of providing all six functions of Marine Air Operations. Compositions based on the tactical situation, the MAGTF's mission and size, and space limitations within the Amphibious Ready Group (ARG).

Lexington Marine praised for his service in Iraq

Lexington resident Betty Carson beams with pride.

Her grandson, Marine Sgt. Terry Carson, has just returned safely from Iraq with a letter of commendation from his commanding officer.

Terry, who grew up in Lexington, is stationed at the Cherry Point Marine Depot in North Carolina. He and his wife Dionne have three children, son Tyler, 4, and daughters Taylor, 3, and Tiffany, 2, and make their home in the Red Bank area.

Carson's commanding officer, Lt. Col. John Torres, wrote his parents, Sandra and Winfred Carson of Lexington, to express his gratitude for their son's contributions to Marine Medium Helicopter Squadron 264.

"The success of the Black Knights would not have been possible without the exceptional efforts of Terry in the Airframes Division," he wrote, "frequently working long hours in a demanding environment."

His squadron conducted combat operations in northern Iraq, a mission off the coast of eastern Africa and a humanitarian mission in the Liberian crisis.

"It is the hard work, total dedication, and commitment of Terry that maintains the legacy of the Marine Corps. I am very proud of his meritorious promotion to the rank of sergeant."

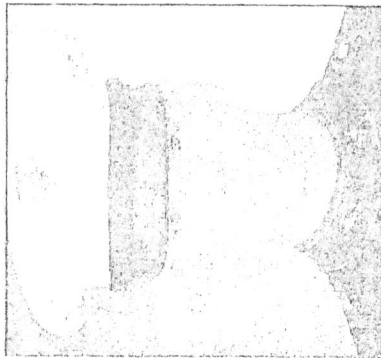
Sgt. Terry Carson

Lexington County Chronicle, SC

January 1, 2005

February 10, 2005

Betty Jewell Durbin, 1949

Doris May Durbin, 1950

Peggy Joyce Durbin, 1953-54

Carol Jean Durbin, 1958-59

BALLARD

The Durbin Branch — June 18, 2005
Durbin Family Reunion — Hutchinson

www.ingramcontent.com/pod-product-compliance
Lightning Source LLC
Chambersburg PA
CBHW080000280326
41935CB00013B/1702